PIGSKIN PARTIES

— BY: —
GENE WESTBROOK

Copyright © 1989
by
Gene Westbrook Publications, Inc.
Millbrook (Montgomery), Alabama
All rights reserved

To Order Additional Books:
****
Pigskin Parties
P.O. Box 869
Millbrook (Montgomery), Alabama 36054
****

First Edition   June 1989   10,000 copies

By GENE WESTBROOK

Cover Design and Illustrations by
GENIA WESTBROOK WOLFE
Recipe Art by JOE WESTBROOK
Editor ISABELLE H. PEAT
Technical assistance by
ALMAND WESTBROOK, JAY WESTBROOK,
JAY WOLFE

Printed in the USA by Rose Printing, Inc.
Box 5078
Tallahassee, Florida 32314

ISBN 0-9614247-1-0   Library of Congress No. 89-050793

About the Artists

Genia Westbrook Wolfe is first and most importantly my daughter. She is a graduate in Visual Art and Design from Auburn University, Auburn, Alabama. Her first endeavor in book design was accomplished while still a student. She designed the cover and divider pages for my first cookbook, *The Magnolia Collection*. Likewise, she has designed the book covers and divider pages for *Pigskin Parties*. Her creative talents provide the visual appeal to Pigskin Parties, and her sense of humor makes the divider pages a treat.

Joe Westbrook is both my husband and my friend. Untiringly, he is my encourager, brainstormer, sounding board, supporter, photographer, book "toter"—the list could go on for pages! Joe's artistic talents are used for the recipe artwork as they were in the first cookbook we published, *The Magnolia Collection*. His wonderful dry wit, along with his artistic talents, comes through on the pages of this book.

About the Technical Assistants

Almand and Jay Westbrook, my college student sons, have attempted to keep me both accurate and knowledgeable on the game of football. This was no easy job! They also had the enviable task of chief tasters and food critics of the recipes used in this cookbook.

Foreword

Well, this is a real "hoot." My position on the football team has always been "quartermaster" not "quarterback." I'm better at getting the game parties together than I am at deciding if the extra point should be kicked or run.

The first ingredient for a great football party is your own cheering section. There must be fans to agree, to argue, to cheer, to grumble, to coach, etc... And then, there must be food and drink to soothe the savage beasts!

Pigskin Parties provides a large selection of recipe choices for tailgating at games, for home parties, and for take-a-long party dishes.

Most importantly, when the play is in motion—on the field or at the party—the name of the game is to HAVE FUN!

Jene

Table of Contents

Appetizers 9-24

Beverages 24-27

Beef 29-38

Pork 39-46

Poultry 47-51

Seafood 52-57

Sandwiches 58-61

Salads and Salad Dressing 63-66

Pasta 67-68

Vegetables 69-76

Eggs and Bread 77-79

Cakes 81-83

Pies 83-84

Cookies 85-87

Desserts 89-91

Index 91-94

Re-order Coupons 95

Acknowledgements

My Very Special Thanks

To my husband, Joe, and our three children, Genia, Almand, and Jay, and our daughter's husband, Jay, for your love, encouragement, enthusiasm, and endurance. You brought this book into being.

To my mother and late father, Gene and Tommy Sparks. You taught me with love how to give a fun-and food-filled party.

To my husband's mother and late stepfather, Ann and Gus Harris, or Pop as we called him. Football parties with all the accompanying excitement and great food were a specialty of theirs.

To all my fun-loving relatives and contributors of recipes: Tommy and Linda Sparks, Scotty Sparks, Lucile Williams, Alice and Jack Roberts, Helen and Grif Carden, Mary and James Keck, Dorothy and Dan Kuerner, Joan and Jim Backes, Bruce and Debby Pfeiffer, Diane and Mike Presley, Woody and Cecelia Pfeiffer, Ellen and Trey Sparks, Elizabeth Sparks Cooper, Beth and Dean Fulghom, Cis and David Godbold, and Velma and Marshall Logan. You give that extra special boost of vitality to the book.

To my carefully chosen friends and contributors of recipes: Betty and Bill Burkett, Alice and Bob Cheers, Joan and the late "Tops" Chew, Jane Dunaway, Jean and Richard Ensley, Ann Gray, Julia Mae Gresham, Leonard Gresham, Marjo and John Gresham, Sal Gresham, Elizabeth and Warren Hall, Elmore Hall, Mitzie and Jack Hinde, Betty House, Beverly and Ron Kuerner, Jo and Mike Mikell, Pat Newsome, Jay and Wanda Payne, Karen and David Rennekamp, Ronee and Gerri from Jacksonville, Jean Segler, Elizabeth Skipper, Patti and John Westrup, Patsy and David Wickmann, and Brad Wolfe. You all know how to "put on a spread."

To my friends that gave support, advice, and encouragement: Carol and Eddie Rees, Dot and Gil Gibson, Leland Eldridge, A. B. and Nancy Carlan, Albert Pence, Claude Leasman, Diane Mayes, Eileen and Mike Green, Debbie and Bob Woodham, Joy Jinks, Pat Bush, Betty Jo Toole, Dot Wainwright, Lucy Glenn, Lynn Carter, Richard Ensley, and John Ray.

Once again to Isabelle Peat for editing *Pigskin Parties*. I more than appreciate all that you do for us! Extra thanks to David and their children for letting me "borrow" some of their time.

All recipes in this book have been made, tested, and enthusiastically enjoyed by my family, friends, and relatives.

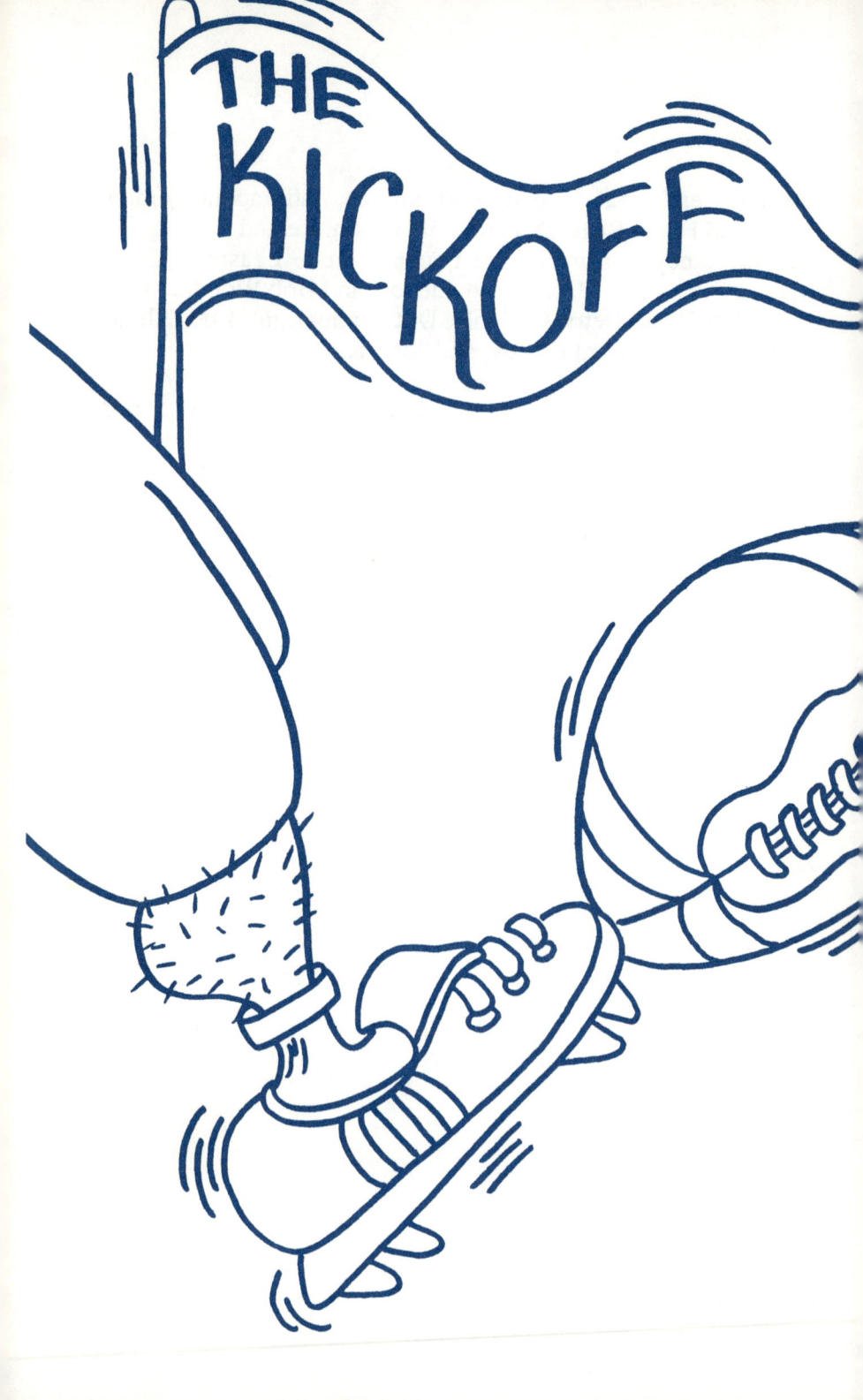

The Kickoff

Baked Brie in Sourdough Bread

1	round loaf sourdough bread, 1 day old	2	cloves garlic, pressed
1/3	cup margarine, melted		1 to 1 1/2 pounds Brie cheese (or Camembert)

Use a serrated knife to hollow-out the bread. Cut a circle through the crust in the top of the round loaf. Slide fingers inside this cut to pull or cut the bread away from the crust leaving a 1/2-inch shell all around. Remove the soft inner bread in one piece, and slice into 1/2-inch thick slices. Mix melted margarine and garlic. Brush inside of the bread bowl with about 3 tablespoons of this mixture. Use the remaining mixture to brush on the soft bread slices. Around the rim of the shell make slits in the crust about 1 1/2 inches apart. Place the cheese, with or without the rind on it, into the bread shell; cut the cheese to fit inside, if needed. Place on a rimmed baking sheet along with the bread slices in a single layer. Bake at 350 degrees until bread slices are toasted, about 10 minutes. Remove the slices to cool. Continue baking the cheese-filled bread bowl until the cut edge is golden brown and the cheese is melted, about 10 more minutes. If using round Brie with the rind on, the cheese will not appear melted after the cooking time until the rind is sliced open. Place the bread bowl on a large platter or wooden board, and surround it with the toasted bread slices. When all the bread slices are eaten, rip into the bread bowl, and use it to dip into the cheese.

Magic!!! No baking dish to clean—it was so good, we ate the bowl.

The Kickoff

Referee Revenge

10	chicken wings	2	tablespoons white vinegar
1/2	cup plain flour		
1-1/8	teaspoons salt, divided	2	tablespoons Tabasco sauce
1/4	teaspoon black pepper		
1/2	teaspoon cayenne pepper	1/4	cup catsup
	Vegetable oil	1/2	cup (1 stick) margarine, melted
2	tablespoons lemon juice		

Disjoint the chicken wings, and discard the bony tips. In a plastic bag, combine flour, 1 teaspoon of the salt, black pepper, and cayenne pepper; shake to mix. Place 4 chicken pieces in the bag; shake to coat. Repeat the process until all chicken is coated. In a large skillet, fry the chicken in 1 inch of oil for about 20 minutes or until chicken is tender and golden brown. Drain chicken on paper towels. In a food processor or blender, blend lemon juice, vinegar, Tabasco sauce, catsup, and remaining 1/8 teaspoon salt; then slowly pour in the melted margarine until the sauce is thick. Pour the sauce over the fried chicken just before serving, or serve the sauce on the side for dipping.

All it takes is one quick glance at the ingredients to know that revenge will be sweet!

The Kickoff

Dorothy's Bison Airfoils!

My husband, Joe, provided the title for his sister's recipe. What a nut—would you have a clue that he's a pilot?

2-1/2 pounds chicken wings   1/2   cup (1 stick) margarine
Vegetable oil   1/4   cup red-hot sauce

Disjoint the chicken wings; discard the bony tips. Fry in hot oil until chicken is done; drain. In a saucepan, melt the margarine, and mix in the hot sauce. Stir the cooked wings into the sauce, and simmer for 5 minutes.

Wow, both this recipe and Referee Revenge on the preceding page are fiery! Referee Revenge is fried with a batter, and Bison Airfoils are fried without batter—your choice. They're both guaranteed to put hair on the chest of a 300-pound tackle!

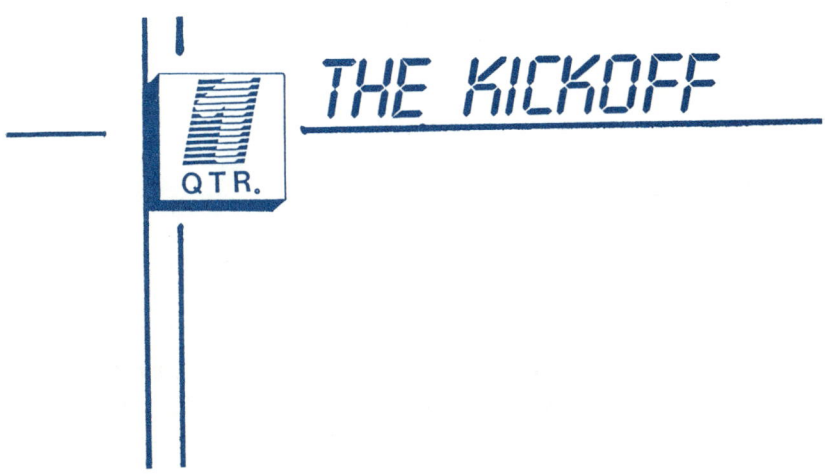

The Kickoff

David's Top-Scoring Mushrooms

2 pounds fresh mushrooms	6 to 8 ounces Swiss cheese, sliced
1/2 cup (1 stick) margarine	6 to 8 ounces sharp Cheddar cheese, sliced
3 cups Burgundy wine	

Remove and discard mushroom stems; then carefully wash the mushroom caps, and drain. In a large skillet, melt the margarine, and add the mushrooms. Stir mushrooms, then add the Burgundy. Allow this "lushy" mixture to simmer for about 20 minutes. Spoon mushrooms into a greased, flat baking dish, using a small amount of the juice. Place the Swiss cheese slices to cover the mushroom caps; then repeat with the Cheddar cheese slices on top of the Swiss cheese. Bake at 350 degrees until all the cheeses are melted and bubbling. Serve with wooden skewers or cocktail forks.

These are also winners as a vegetable side dish. You may need more Burgundy for the mushrooms if the mushrooms are large and "thirsty." You may need some, too, if you're "thirsty"!

Holy Smoke!

- 1 pound wieners
- 1 large (15-1/2-ounce) bottle Pepperoncini (mild Greek peppers)

Cut the wieners into 1-inch chunks, and place in a saucepan. Empty the entire bottle of juice and peppers into the pan. Heat to a boil; reduce heat, and simmer for 15 minutes. Serve warm. This can be cooled and refrigerated for several days.

Super easy to make—lightly hot and spicy.

The Kickoff

Texas Crabgrass

1	10-ounce package frozen chopped spinach	1	(6-ounce) can crabmeat, drained
1/4	cup (1/2 stick) margarine	3/4	cup Parmesan cheese, grated
1	medium onion, chopped very fine	1/4	cup cooking sherry

Thaw spinach completely; then squeeze all the water out. In a skillet, melt margarine, and saute the onions. Add the spinach, and continue to saute for about 5 minutes. Mix in the remaining ingredients, and stir until all ingredients are well blended and very hot. Serve hot in a chafing dish with crackers.

Looks like it sounds! Tastes fantastic.

The Kickoff

Coins for the Toss by Joan

1/2 cup (1 stick) margarine, softened	1/2 teaspoon crushed oregano
2 ounces Mozzarella cheese, grated	1/2 teaspoon seasoned salt
1/4 cup grated Parmesan cheese	Dash cayenne pepper
1 cup plain flour	1 ounce pepperoni, ground

In a large bowl, combine the softened margarine, Mozzarella cheese, and Parmesan cheese until blended. Add flour, oregano, seasoned salt, and cayenne pepper; mix to blend. Add ground pepperoni, and mix well. Divide dough in half, and place on waxed paper; shape into two 6-inch rolls. Wrap the rolls in the waxed paper, and chill for several hours or overnight. To bake, preheat oven to 375 degrees. Slice dough into 1/4-inch slices, and bake on a greased cookie sheet for 10 to 12 minutes. Transfer to a wire rack to cool. Yield: 50.

Clock-Stopper Chicken Tidbits

2 pounds boneless chicken breasts, skinned	1 cup Parmesan cheese, grated
1 bottle Italian dressing	
3 cups Italian-style bread crumbs	

Cut chicken breasts into bite-size pieces, and place in a glass bowl. Pour on the Italian dressing, and toss to coat the pieces. Cover and refrigerate for 3 to 6 hours. In a bowl, combine the bread crumbs and Parmesan cheese. Drain chicken; then roll in the crumb mixture. Place tidbits on an ungreased cookie sheet in a single layer. Bake in a preheated oven at 400 degrees until done and browned, about 10 to 12 minutes.

The Kickoff

Looks Bad Tastes Great Dip by Betty

Make at least one day in advance of serving. It can be made several days earlier and refrigerated. Add the almonds and cheese just before serving.

1	pound lean ground beef	1	teaspoon salt
1	small onion, chopped	1	teaspoon pepper
2	cloves garlic, minced	1/2	teaspoon oregano
3/4	cup pimento, chopped	3/4	cup slivered almonds, toasted
1	(10-ounce) can Ro-Tel tomatos and green chilies	8	ounces Velvetta cheese, cubed
1	(4-ounce) can chopped black olives		
1	(4-ounce) can mushrooms, drained and chopped		

In a large skillet, brown the ground beef, and drain the excess drippings. Add all of the remaining ingredients except the almonds and cheese; mix well. Allow the mixture to simmer very slowly for 2 hours. Just before serving, add the cheese cubes; stir until cheese is melted. Mix in the toasted almonds. Serve in a chafing dish or other warming pot with round tortilla chips or crackers.

This is really a Picadillo dip without the golden raisins. If you'd like to add them for authenticity, use about 3/4 cup golden raisins. Tommy and Linda were right—it does taste great!

The Kickoff

Prairie Fire

2	(15-ounce) cans pinto beans	1	bunch green onions, chopped (including tops)
1	cup (2 sticks) margarine		
2	cups sharp Cheddar cheese, grated	1	large clove garlic, minced
1/2	cup pickled Jalapeno peppers, chopped		Round, thin tortilla chips
1	teaspoon Jalapeno pepper juice		Extra green onions for garnish

Drain and mash the pinto beans. In a saucepan, mix all ingredients except the chips. Heat on medium until the cheese has melted and the mixture is bubbling. Serve hot in a chafing dish or crock pot with the chips on the side. Garnish with the extra green onions.

This can also be made in the microwave. Use a glass or microwave dish with a lid; heat until bubbling. Open microwave; stir mixture and turn the dish. Microwave again until bubbling.

If you like it hot—great! Otherwise, you may want a bucket of water brought in from the sidelines.

Short Punts

50	small scallops	2	tablespoons vegetable oil
25	slices bacon, cut in half		Cocktail picks, natural color

Place each scallop on a bacon half, and roll. Secure the bacon with a cocktail pick. In a large skillet, saute the rolled scallops in hot oil until the bacon is very crisp. Drain on paper towel. Serve hot.

The Kickoff

Almand's Forward Pass Spread

1	(14-ounce) can sauerkraut, well drained and chopped	2	tablespoons chopped pimentos
4	ounces sharp Cheddar cheese, finely grated	2	tablespoons minced parsley
5	ounces finely chopped turkey ham	1	tablespoon minced onion
1/2	cup mayonnaise	1	cup sour cream
14	saltine crackers, finely crushed		

Additional sharp Cheddar cheese, finely grated
Whole pimento strips

In a large bowl, mix sauerkraut, cheese, turkey ham, mayonnaise, crackers, chopped pimentos, parsley, and onion. When all ingredients are well mixed, shape the mixture into a mound on a flat plate. Spread the sour cream evenly over the entire mound; chill. Just before serving, garnish with the additional finely grated cheese to lightly cover the mound. Use the pimento strips to write the team's letter symbols.

Rah Rah's

Make these early in the day. The sauce tastes best after being blended for a few hours.

1	cup catsup	1	cup bourbon
1	cup brown sugar	3	pounds wieners, cut into bite-size pieces
1/3	cup soy sauce		

In a saucepan, mix together the catsup, brown sugar, soy sauce, and bourbon. Bring to a boil, and add the cut wieners; reduce heat, and simmer for about 20 minutes. Remove from heat, and cool. Place in a glass jar with a tight-fitting lid, and refrigerate until serving time. At serving time, heat and serve in a chafing dish or other warming-type vessel.

The Kickoff

Brandied Shrimp

The shrimp can be cooked as instructed below, or use shrimp that is already cooked.

1 pound medium-to-large shrimp, shelled	1/2 cup mayonnaise
2 to 4 tablespoons margarine	1/4 cup Half and Half
Salt	1/4 cup catsup
Black pepper	1/4 teaspoon Worcestershire sauce
Juice of one large lemon	1 ounce brandy

Wash shrimp in 6 different rinses of cold water; drain. In a skillet, saute the shrimp in the margarine until all of the shrimp are completely pink in color. Salt and pepper to taste. Refrigerate the shrimp to chill. In a small bowl, mix the lemon juice, mayonnaise, Half and Half, catsup, and Worcestershire sauce until blended. Stir in the brandy last. Serve in individual shrimp cocktail bowls with the sauce spooned over the shrimp.

This recipe can also used for a party with the shrimp in a larger bowl over ice and the sauce on the side for dipping. Or the sauce can be mixed with all the shrimp and served in a lettuce-lined bowl.

Elmore's Surprise Wraps

1 (15-1/2-ounce) can unsweetened pineapple chunks or fresh pineapple chunks	1 package extra lean sliced bacon Cocktail picks

Drain the pineapple; then wrap each chunk in 1/3 slice of bacon. Secure with a cocktail pick. Place the bacon-wrapped chunks on a microwave dish covered with paper towel. Place paper towel on top of the chunks; microwave until the bacon is lightly crisp.

The Kickoff

Scallop Ceviche

The lime juice "cooks" the scallops.

- 1 cup fresh raw small bay scallops (larger can be used)
- 1/2 cup fresh lime juice
- 3 tablespoons onion, minced
- 2 tablespoons green pepper, minced
- 1 tablespoon parsley, minced
- 1 small clove garlic, split
- 2 drops Tabasco sauce
- 3 tablespoons vegetable or olive oil
- Salt to taste
- Pepper to taste

If scallops are large, cut into bite-size pieces. Place scallops in a glass bowl; then pour on the lime juice, and toss to mix. Cover and refrigerate overnight; stir several times during the marinating time. In the morning, stir in the remaining ingredients, and allow to marinate several more hours. Drain before serving, and remove the garlic piece. Serve cold with crackers.

Pecan Confetti

- 1 (8-ounce) package cream cheese, softened
- 2 tablespoons milk
- 1/2 cup sour cream
- 1/3 cup minced green pepper
- 1/4 cup minced green onions, including tops
- 1 tablespoon Worcestershire sauce
- 1/4 teaspoon garlic powder
- 1/4 teaspoon salt
- 1/8 teaspoon black pepper
- 1 (2-1/2-ounce) jar dried beef, minced
- 1 cup pecans, chopped

Combine the softened cream cheese with the milk; then blend in the sour cream. Add the remaining ingredients except the pecans; mix well. Pour into a greased 9-inch pie plate, and sprinkle with the chopped pecans. Bake at 350 degrees for 20 minutes. Serve on melba rounds.

The Kickoff

Quesadillas Caliente

10 (7 to 8-inch) flour tortillas
Taco sauce; hot, medium, or mild
2-1/2 cups sharp Cheddar cheese, grated

Brush 5 tortillas with water on both sides, and place on an ungreased cookie sheet. Spread on about 1/2 to 1 teaspoon of the taco sauce; then sprinkle with 1/2 cup of the cheese on each tortilla. Top with another tortilla. Brush the tortilla with water; then cover the pan with aluminum foil. Bake at 300 degrees for about 10 minutes, or until cheese is melted. Remove from the oven, and cut into 6 wedges. Serve hot. Yield: 30 wedges.

These can also be made with thin slices of cheese rather than grated cheese. Try different amounts and temperatures of taco sauce to suit your taste.

Monterey Quesadillas

10 (7 to 8-inch) flour tortillas
2-1/2 cups Monterey Jack cheese, grated
1 (4-ounce) can chopped green chilies
1 (2-1/4-ounce) can chopped ripe olives

Brush 5 tortillas with water on both sides, and place on an ungreased cookie sheet. Sprinkle 1/2 cup of the cheese on each tortilla; then sprinkle with chopped green chilies and chopped ripe olives. Top each with another tortilla. Brush the tortilla with water; then cover the pan with aluminum foil. Bake at 300 degrees for about 10 minutes, or until cheese is melted. Remove from the oven, and cut into 6 wedges. Serve hot. Yield: 30 wedges.

The Kickoff

Salsa Verde

These salsas are very versatile. Use either of the two salsas on tacos, as a dip, on top of omelettes, scrambled eggs, huevos rancheros (see Eggs), hamburgers, hot dogs, etc. The salsas can be refrigerated in a tightly covered container for several days, or they can be frozen.

- 1 tablespoon margarine
- 1/2 cup onion, minced
- 2 tablespoons flour
- 1-1/2 cups chicken broth
- 1 (4-ounce) can chopped green chilies
- 1 clove garlic, minced
- 3/4 teaspoon salt
- Scant 1/4 teaspoon cumin
- 2 tablespoons vinegar
- Tabasco sauce to desired temperature!

In a large skillet, melt margarine, and add onions; saute until translucent. Stir in the flour until smooth. Mix in all remaining ingredients, and simmer for 20 minutes.

Red Salsa

Use the same recipe as Salsa Verde (see recipe above) with this exception: use 2 cups stewed tomatoes instead of the chicken broth.

The Kickoff

Jean's Chinese Pecans

4	cups pecans	Vegetable oil
1/2	cup sugar	Salt
1	teaspoon crushed red pepper	

Place pecans in a saucepan with enough water to cover; boil for 1 minute. Drain in a colander. Mix sugar and red pepper together in a large bowl; toss the pecans in the mixture. Place a slotted spoon near the cooking area. In a large skillet, heat 1 inch of oil until hot, but not smoking; fry pecans until golden brown. Drain the fried pecans in a colander that has paper towel under it to catch excess oil. Place the hot, drained pecans on waxed paper (do not use paper towel), and sprinkle with salt.

Fabulous! It's a strange mixture of ingredients and instructions that has an outstanding outcome.

Goal Line Wings

Marinate overnight.

12	chicken wings		1/4	cup lemon juice
1/2	cup soy sauce		2	cloves garlic, mashed
1	tablespoon brown sugar		3	drops Tabasco sauce
3/4	cup catsup			

Disjoint the chicken wings, and use only the meaty 2 pieces (drumettes). Place the drumettes in a flat baking dish. Mix together all of the remaining ingredients, and pour over the chicken. Cover, and refrigerate overnight; turn the drumettes occasionally. Remove the chicken from the marinade, and bake at 350 degrees for 15 minutes; then broil at 500 degrees for an additional 5 minutes. Yield: 24.

The Kickoff

First Downers

1/2	cup margarine (1 stick), melted	2	teaspoons seasoned salt
1/2	teaspoon onion powder	1	loaf fresh Italian or French bread, sliced lengthwise
2	teaspoons lemon juice		
2	teaspoons poppy seeds	3/4 to 1 pound Swiss cheese, grated	
2	teaspoons Dijon mustard		

Melt margarine; add onion powder, lemon juice, poppy seeds, mustard, and seasoned salt. Mix to blend well. Spread 1/2 of this mixture on each half of bread. Top the margarine mixture with the grated cheese. Place both halves of bread side by side on aluminum foil; do not cover. Bake at 350 degrees for 20 minutes. Cut into bite-size pieces to serve warm.

This can be made several days in advance. Wrap very tightly in aluminum foil, and freeze, unbaked. Remove from freezer, and allow to thaw before baking. Don't forget to bake uncovered!

Wilson's Popcorn Bowl

1	cup Parmesan cheese, grated	1/4	teaspoon dry mustard
1-1/2	teaspoons garlic powder	1/8	teaspoon sugar
2-1/2	teaspoons salt	Hot popcorn	
1	teaspoon black pepper	Margarine	

In a large salt shaker that has large holes, mix the cheese, garlic powder, salt, black pepper, mustard, and sugar until blended. Shake this mixture over your hot, buttered popcorn.

If there is some left, use it on salads or on cooked vegetables.

The Kickoff

Mary's Mystery Crab and Shrimp

Make one day before serving.

4	hard boiled eggs, peeled and chopped	1	(6-ounce) can shrimp, chilled and drained
12	slices white sandwich bread, crusts removed and bread cubed	1	cup celery, cut fine
		1-1/2	cups mayonnaise
1	large onion, chopped	1	tablespoon lemon juice
1	(6-ounce) can crabmeat, chilled and drained		Salt to taste

Combine chopped eggs, bread cubes, and onions in a glass bowl; refrigerate, tightly covered, overnight. The next day, add the remaining ingredients, and salt to taste. Keep refrigerated. Yield: 1 quart.

This is intriguing for both the ingredients and the variety of ways to serve. It can be used as a spread on crackers or melba toast, as a salad served on a bed of lettuce, or as a sandwich spread. Keep 'em guessing about what's in it—that adds to the mystery.

Jay's Instant Replay

1/3	cup Myer's dark rum or vodka	4	large strawberries, hulled and washed
1	cup orange juice		Juice of 1/2 large lemon
2/3	cup apple juice	1/4	cup tonic water

In a blender, mix all ingredients. Serve over ice cubes. Serves 3 to 4.

Delicious concoction that is not too sweet—jussst right!! Keep the blender handy; there'll be calls for a replay.

The Kickoff

Jay Scott's Straight-Down-the-Middle Breezie

2	ounces Vodka	2	ounces club soda
3	ounces orange juice	Ice cubes	
3	ounces pineapple juice		

In a 12-ounce glass, mix Vodka, orange juice, and pineapple juice until well blended. Stir in the club soda and ice cubes.

Great way to get your Vitamin C!

Polar Pick-Me-Up

1-1/4 ounces Gin		1	ounce unsweetened
1/2	ounce Triple Sec		pineapple juice
1/2	ounce lemon juice	Ice	

In a shaker, mix all ingredients; shake thoroughly to blend, and chill. Strain into a pre-chilled champagne glass.

This recipe was given to me by our friends Patti and John, from the frozen north of Canada. It'll cool your throat and warm your cleats.

Red River Red-Eye

Tomato juice
Beer ... Canadian of course!

In a tall, cold glass, mix ingredients in the proportions of 1/3 tomato juice to 2/3 beer.

Of course, this was given to me by our Canadian friends. Who else is hearty enough to drink the stuff?

The Kickoff

Hail Caesar !!

1/2 ounce lemon juice	Pepper
5 drops Worcestershire sauce	1-1/2 ounces Vodka
	Ice cubes
2 drops Tabasco sauce	Celery ribs, with leaves on and washed
Mott's Clamato juice	
Salt	Salt rims of glasses (optional)

To salt a glass rim: use 1/2 lemon to moisten the rim of the glass. Pour a generous amount of salt into a flat dish. Invert the glass into the salt, and twist to coat rim with salt.

In a 10-ounce glass, mix lemon juice, Worcestershire sauce, and Tabasco until well blended. Add Clamato juice to fill glass 2/3 full; season to taste with salt and pepper. Add Vodka, stir; then fill glass with ice cubes. Place a rib of celery in the glass for a stirrer.

Spicy and refreshing!

Canadian Coffee

Heat resistant stemmed glass	1-1/2 ounces Canadian Club
1/2 fresh lemon	Sweetened whipped cream
Granulated white sugar	1 tablespoon chocolate liqueur
Hot coffee	
1 ounce orange liqueur	

Run the cut edge of the lemon around the edge of the glass; then invert into a saucer of the sugar, and twist to coat the rim. Fill glass 2/3 full with hot coffee. Carefully stir in the orange liqueur, and the Canadian Club. Top with a dollop of whipped cream; then drizzle the chocolate liqueur over the cream.

That'll warm ya' like a fast sprint on a cold day.

The Kickoff

Personal "Fowl"

1-1/2 ounces Wild Turkey
1-1/2 ounces Amaretto
3 to 4 ounces cola
Ice

Mix Wild Turkey and Amaretto in a tall glass. Add the cola, and fill glass with ice.

This'll knock your helmet off.

Top Scorers

Quarterback Club Steaks

Steaks
Salt
Cracked black pepper

This is a "how-to" cook steaks recipe. Cooking a really good, juicy steak is a true art form, just like planning game strategy. Here are a few tips:

* Select a tender cut, such as a T-bone, rib-eye, Delmonico, filet mignon, porterhouse, N.Y. strip, or sirloin. Have it cut about 1 to 1-1/2 inches thick.

* For outstanding pure steak flavor, do nothing to the meat (no spice or marinade).

* Remove steaks from refrigeration about 1/2 hour before cooking time.

* Use a charcoal or gas grill.

* Have the fire hot, but not flaming.

* Place steaks over direct fire on the grill, and allow to sear. Then pull cover over grill, and watch the flames to prevent burning.

* Cook about 5 minutes; then turn steaks. Sear, and cook another 5 minutes.

(continued on next page)

Top Scorers

* With a knife, make a small slit to the center of a steak to test for desired doneness. Do not pierce the meat any more than necessary. Piercing causes the meat to lose juices.

* Remove steaks from grill when they reach a slightly pinker color than desired, since the meat will continue to cook for a short time.

* Place steaks on a warm platter, and immediately sprinkle salt and pepper on both sides of the meat. Do not wait even a few minutes to season, since the meat begins to seal as it cools.

All of this seems long-winded, but truly great steaks are as sought-after as a fumbled ball at the goal line.

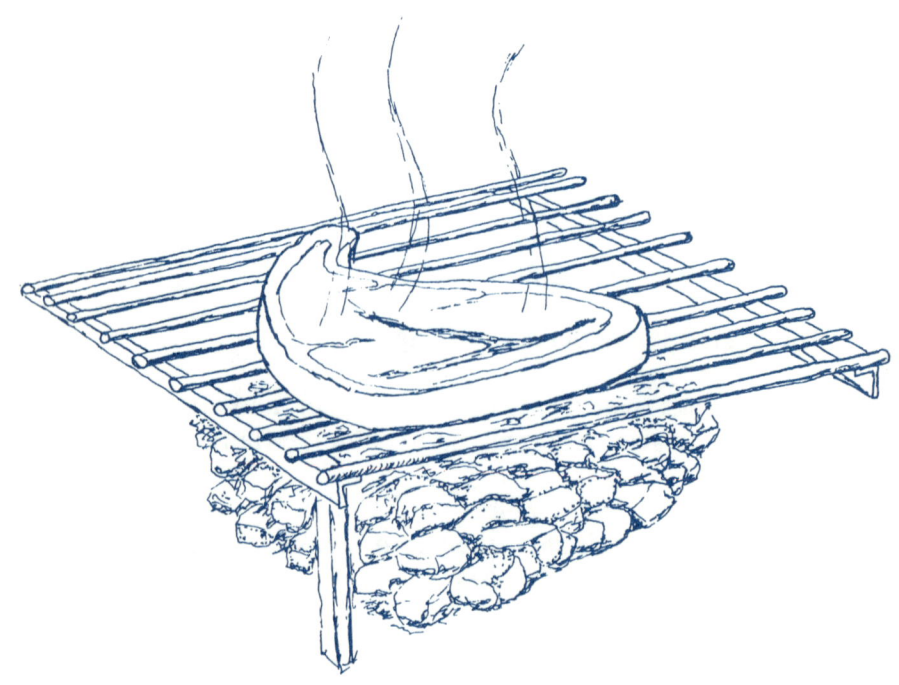

Top Scorers

Hula Steaks

Steaks require overnight marination.

4	steaks, tender cut about 1-inch thick	2	tablespoons cooking sherry (optional)
1	20-ounce can pineapple slices, liquid reserved	1/2	teaspoon ground ginger
2/3	cup soy sauce (lite soy can be used)	1	large clove garlic, minced

Place steaks in a glass baking dish. In a small bowl, combine pineapple liquid, soy sauce, sherry, ginger, and garlic; mix well. (Eat the pineapple slices since the juice is all you need.) Pour the marinade over the steaks, and turn steaks once. Cover and refrigerate overnight; turn the steaks once again after a few hours of marination. Remove steaks from the marinade 1/2 hour before cooking. Grill directly over hot coals for 5 minutes; turn and grill for another 5 minutes. Make a small slit in the center of one steak to check for desired doneness. Remove steaks from grill when still slightly pinker than desired since steaks continue to cook for a short time. Add salt only if needed. Serves 4.

Top Scorers

Over-the-Top Steak

1-1/2 to 2-pounds round steak, 1-inch thick	1 tablespoon Worcestershire sauce
1/4 cup plain flour	8 ounces whole, small fresh mushrooms (washed and stems removed)
1 teaspoon salt	
1/4 teaspoon black pepper	
1 teaspoon dry mustard	
2 tablespoons vegetable oil	4 tablespoons margarine
1/2 cup water	Garlic salt to taste

Pound the steak to flatten and tenderize. In a small bowl, combine the flour, salt, pepper, and mustard. Rub this mixture into both sides of the steak. In a large skillet, brown the steak in the hot oil on both sides. In a cup, mix the water and Worcestershire sauce; pour over the steak. Cover the skillet, and allow the steak to simmer for 1-1/2 hours. During the last 10 minutes of cooking time, use a small skillet to saute the mushrooms in the margarine. Sprinkle with garlic salt to taste. Place the steak on a warm platter, and cover with the mushrooms. Pour any sauce left in the steak pan over the top of the mushrooms and steak. Serves 4 to 6.

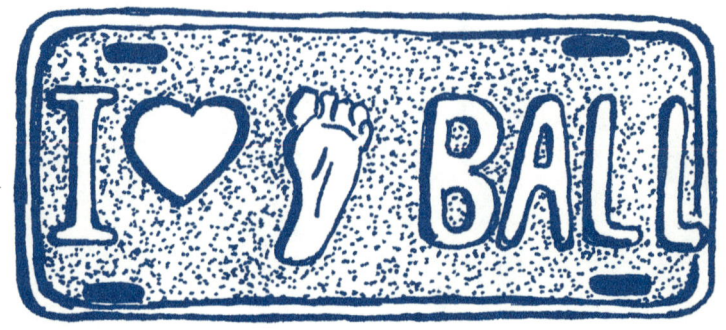

Top Scorers

Hit-'em-a-Lick Steak

1-1/2	pounds round steak, 1-inch thick	2	cups tomatoes, chopped
2	tablespoons plain flour	2	teaspoons Worcestershire sauce
1	teaspoon salt	1	teaspoon dry mustard
1/8	teaspoon black pepper	1/2	teaspoon chili powder
2	tablespoons vegetable oil	1	whole bay leaf
2	medium onions, sliced in rings		

Pound the steak to flatten and tenderize. In a small bowl, combine the flour, salt, and pepper; rub into both sides of the steak. In a large skillet, brown the steak on both sides in the hot oil. Remove skillet from heat, and place the onion rings on the steak. In a bowl, combine the remaining ingredients, and blend. Pour the sauce over the steak and onions. Cover and cook over low heat for about 1-1/2 hours, or until tender. Serves 4 to 6.

Scrimmage Line Steak

2	pounds round steak, cut 1-1/2 inches thick	1	cup water
		4	tablespoons chili sauce
1	tablespoon prepared mustard	1	teaspoon Worcestershire sauce
1	teaspoon salt	1/2	teaspoon paprika
1/4	teaspoon black pepper	2	tablespoons chopped onion
2	tablespoons plain flour		
3	tablespoons vegetable oil		

Score the beef on both sides; then spread mustard on both sides. Salt and pepper the beef, and sprinkle with the flour. In a large skillet, heat oil; then brown the beef on both sides. Carefully pour in the water; add the remaining ingredients, and blend well. Bring sauce to a boil; reduce heat to simmer, and cover. Simmer for 1-1/2 hours. Serves 6.

Top Scorers

First and Ten Spaghetti

This one is a tried-and-true approach that needs to be used several times each season since it'll always make your goal of a super supper.

1-1/2	pounds extra lean ground beef	1	(15-ounce) can tomato sauce
1	cup onions, chopped	1/2	tablespoon oregano, crushed
1	clove garlic, minced		
1	teaspoon salt	1	teaspoon garlic salt
1	(28-ounce) can tomatoes, chopped	1/8	teaspoon black pepper
		3	drops Tabasco sauce

In a large cooking pot, brown ground beef, onions, and garlic, crumbling the meat while cooking. Add the remaining ingredients, and stir to blend. Bring to a boil; then reduce heat to simmer. Cook, uncovered, for 2-1/2 hours. Do not shorten the cooking time. Skim any extra oil from the top of the pot. The pasta cooking instructions follow on the next page. Serves 6.

This is a fantastic spaghetti sauce. For years I used to ad-lib my spaghetti sauce—sometimes it was outstanding, and sometimes I'd missed the goal by the proverbial "country mile." Finally I settled on this recipe, which sends it right between the poles every time.

The sauce can be frozen for a couple of months, or it can be refrigerated for several days. I find that it's easiest to make either early in the morning and let it simmer for the 2-1/2 hours, or make it after dinner and let it simmer while I'm relaxing. Curious, I wonder why I don't ever make it during the day?

Top Scorers

Cooking the Pasta

Water
Salt

Pasta or noodles
1 tablespoon margarine

Personally, I prefer the vermicelli noodles. You can also use the spaghetti noodles, which are slightly thicker, or the linguine noodles, which are thicker and flat rather than round. Fill a large pot with water; add salt and bring to a boil. Add noodles a few at a time, either whole or broken in half, and stir. Add a tablespoon of margarine or oil to the boiling water to prevent the noodles from sticking together. Bring water and noodles back to a boil; cover with a tight lid, and turn heat off. Leave pot on burner, and let it remain there for exactly 9 minutes. Test for doneness since the thicker noodles may require another minute or two cooking time. Drain, but do not rinse noodles. Serve with the sauce immediately.

There are several tricks to good pasta that I'd like to pass on to you. First, I don't know how to measure the pasta, either. Your guess is surely as good or better than mine. Next, use plenty of water to cook the pasta. Have enough salt to give the noodles good flavor. Do not overcook pasta; it is very important to have the noodles just "al dente." Mushy pasta is really "out." Also don't rinse the noodles and wash off the flavor. If you have to cook the pasta and wait before serving it, add extra margarine to the drained noodles, and toss well to prevent the noodles from sticking together. There seems to be a lot of "don'ts" in here—DO enjoy it.

Top Scorers

Joe's Favorite Wild and Wooly Chili

3	pounds round steak or roast	14	ounces water
2	tablespoons vegetable oil	3	teaspoons beef bouillon
3	cloves garlic, minced	1/4	teaspoon black pepper
5	tablespoons chili powder (yes, tablespoons)	1	(15-ounce) can pinto beans (optional)
2	teaspoons ground cumin		Tortilla chips (optional)
3	tablespoons plain flour		Grated Cheddar cheese (optional)
1	tablespoon crushed oregano		Minced onion (optional)
3	(10-1/2-ounce) cans beef consomme		

Cut beef into bite-size pieces after trimming off all fat. In a large pot, heat oil and stir in the beef pieces until the meat changes color but does not brown. Lower heat, and stir in garlic. In a small bowl, mix together chili powder, cumin, flour, and oregano until well blended. Sprinkle the flour mixture over the meat, and stir to coat. Slowly add the consomme; stir to mix. Then blend in the water, bouillion, and pepper. Simmer, uncovered, for 20 minutes. Add beans, if desired, and simmer another 10 minutes. Serve chili in a bowl plain, or over tortilla chips in a bowl topped with either cheese, onion, or both.

True, this seems like a strange chili without onions or tomatoes in it. Regardless, everyone around here requests it often, football games or not!

Top Scorers

Cis's Quick Crockpot Camp Stew

1	pound extra lean ground beef	1	(16-ounce) can small green peas, drained (optional)
2	(5-ounce) cans Swanson's white chicken meat, chunk style	2	(16-ounce) cans whole white potatoes, drained and cut into cubes
1	(15-ounce) can Castleberry's barbecue pork	1	(14-ounce) bottle hot catsup
1	(17-ounce) can cream-style corn	1	large onion, chopped
1	(12-ounce) can white shoepeg corn, drained	2	tablespoons Worcestershire sauce
1	(17-ounce) can green lima beans, drained		

In a skillet, cook and crumble the ground beef until browned; drain. Place all of the ingredients in a crockpot on high for 1-1/2 hours; then turn the temperature to low until ready to serve.

Top Scorers

Ann's Homemade Chili

1-1/2 pounds extra lean ground beef	2 (16-ounce) cans tomatoes
1-1/2 teaspoons salt	1-1/2 ounces chili powder
3 onions, chopped	2 tablespoons plain flour
2 tablespoons vegetable oil	Water

In a Dutch oven, brown the ground beef, and crumble the meat while cooking. Pour off any excess drippings, and stir salt into the meat. In a skillet, saute the onions in the oil until tender. Stir the cooked onions into the meat. Drain the tomato liquid from the cans into the meat mixture; then chop the tomatoes before adding to the sauce. Measure the chili powder into a cup; add the flour and enough water to make a paste. Stir paste until smooth, and thin with enough water to pour into the sauce. Stir to blend all ingredients; bring sauce to a boil. Reduce heat to simmer, and cook for 45 minutes.

This is a great mild chili to serve on a cold day. It also is fantastic as a topping for hot dogs with chopped onions.

Top Scorers

Barbecue for the Fans

Depending on the number of fans you are feeding, select one of the choices below:

One (or more) whole, uncured hams
Half an uncured ham

Pork loin roast
Boston butt, as lean as possible

Using a slightly educated guess here, since there are a lot of variables, cook the meat over indirect coals for approximately 30 to 45 minutes per pound. The meat can be cooked covered or uncovered. Immediately after removing from heat, salt the meat over the entire surface. Leave the meat whole until just before serving; then either chop or shred the pork after discarding the fat. The pork can be cooled, wrapped in plastic wrap, and refrigerated until time to cut it. Shortly before serving time, allow the meat to come to room temperature. Do not heat the meat; serve room temperature with a sauce that is bubbling hot. Do not leave any meat unrefrigerated for a long time.

This can be served as a meat with a piping hot sauce by itself, or it can be served on a heated bun with the hot sauce. Use the **Quick Barbecue Sauce,** *allowing it to simmer for about 8 minutes. The sauce can be cooled, bottled, and refrigerated until time to reheat for serving.*

Quick Barbecue Sauce

2 cups catsup
1/2 cup vinegar
1 teaspoon garlic salt

1/2 cup soy sauce (can use lite soy)

Mix all ingredients in a saucepan. Do not cook if using on meat that is being cooked with the sauce on it. Otherwise, allow sauce to come to a boil; then reduce heat to a simmer. Cook for about 8 minutes.

Top Scorers

Running Back Ribs

Select the ribs with the most meat on them. There are several names of cuts to use—pork fingers, fingerlings, country backbone, spareribs, etc. Regardless of the name, ribs are best when cooked slowly. Build your fire with enough charcoal to last for a while, and only on one side of the pit. Allow coals to get hot, and have a grey ash on them. Place the ribs on the other side of the grill so that no part of the meat is directly over the coals. Pull the lid to the grill down, and adjust vents to cook ribs slowly but steadily. Cook for about 2 hours; then dip the ribs into the saucepan to cover with sauce. Allow ribs to cook a short time longer on the grill until the sauce has set. You never have to worry about the ribs or sauce burning when cooked this way.

Long Pass Barbecue Sauce

1/2	cup catsup	2	tablespoons lemon juice
1/2	cup onion, chopped	1	teaspoon prepared mustard
1	large clove garlic, minced		
1/4	cup vegetable oil	1	teaspoon salt
1	(16-ounce) can applesauce	1/2	teaspoon ground ginger
2	tablespoons honey	1/4	teaspoon black pepper
1	tablespoon Worcestershire sauce	4	drops Tabasco sauce

In a saucepan, mix all ingredients, and bring to boil. Reduce heat to a simmer, and cook for about 20 minutes. Serves as a sauce for ribs, pork roast, or chicken.

Top Scorers

Pop's Lazy Acres Bar-B-Que Sauce

1 quart vinegar	1/2 cup (1 stick) margarine, melted
4 large onions, chopped	
2 or 3 lemons, halved	1 cup water
1/3 cup Lea and Perrins Worcestershire sauce	5 cloves garlic, minced
	Tabasco sauce, "a couple of good dashes"
3/4 cup soy sauce	
1 ounce chili powder	28 ounces catsup
4 tablespoons prepared mustard	

In a large saucepan, add vinegar, onions, and lemons. Cook until onions are tender. Lift the lemons out of the sauce, and squeeze the juice back into the sauce. Add all remaining ingredients except the catsup, and simmer for 10 minutes. Stir in the catsup, and cook until thickened.

Man, is this sauce good on grilled chickens or ribs! Just the taste of it brings back waves of memories of great times at Lazy Acres. When Pop was barbecuing during football games, you could count on a cheering crowd. Every radio and television was turned on to catch the different angles of play and all the play-by-play commentary. My favorite story along these lines is of Joe's younger sisters asking their mother in September if she had anything to tell Pop before January because he'd be busy with his games 'til then!! He was a dyed-in-the wool football fan.

Top Scorers

Bar-B-Que Brisket by Beverly

Brisket:

1	5-pound beef brisket, trimmed of excess fat
2	teaspoons garlic salt
2	teaspoons onion salt
2	teaspoons celery salt
1	onion, minced
3 to 5	tablespoons liquid smoke
1	(5-ounce) bottle Worcestershire sauce
1/4	teaspoon black pepper

Place brisket in a 9x13-inch glass baking dish, fat side down. Sprinkle with all ingredients except Worcestershire sauce and pepper. Cover with plastic wrap, and refrigerate overnight. Before cooking, preheat oven to 275 degrees; then pour the Worcestershire sauce on the brisket, and sprinkle with the pepper. Cover with foil, and bake for 6 hours. After cooking, remove brisket from sauce, and shred or slice the meat.

Sauce:

1	(32-ounce) bottle catsup
2	cups water
1/4	cup brown sugar
1/4	cup Worcestershire sauce
1	teaspoon garlic salt
2	tablespoons vinegar
1/4	teaspoon Tabasco sauce
1	teaspoon dry mustard
1	teaspoon chili powder
1	teaspoon liquid smoke or more if preferred
1/4	teaspoon ground red pepper
1-1/4	teaspoon black pepper

In a large saucepan, combine all ingredients. Cook, uncovered, over medium heat for about 20 minutes. Pour 2 cups of the hot sauce over the hot shredded brisket. Serve on warm buns with extra sauce on the side. Cool, bottle, and refrigerate the remaining sauce. Sauce keeps well in the refrigerator, or can be frozen. Yield: 6 cups sauce.

Top Scorers

Stick to 'Ya Ribs Linebacker Soup

6	medium Idaho potatoes, cooked in salted water, peeled, and cubed
8	green onions, sliced (including green tops)
2	medium onions, chopped
1-1/2	quarts chicken broth or stock
6	ounces cream cheese, softened

Salt
4 drops Tabasco sauce
1-1/2 pounds Polish or hickory smoked sausage, cooked, drained, and sliced in rounds
Paprika

In a large pot, add cooked potatoes, green onions, chopped onions, and chicken broth. Bring to a boil; then reduce heat to simmer, and cook 45 minutes. Place the potato mixture in a food processor with the steel blade or in a blender or mixer; then add the cream cheese, cut in chunks, and puree until smooth. Add salt to taste and Tabasco sauce. Return soup to the pot to reheat. Add the cooked, sliced sausage, and stir until the soup is hot. Serve hot with the paprika sprinkled on top for color. Serves 8 or more.

This one will really warm you all the way down to your shinpads. It's thick, rich, hearty, and deee-licious.

Ahhh! Pizzas

How can you miss with a pizza party? Pizzas are always perfect. You can serve them in hot, cold, or mild weather. They can be made to suit almost anyone's taste buds by varying the ingredients used to top the pizza. And the aroma while they bake is enough to make a die-hard football fan wish for halftime!

There are plenty of different approaches to a pizza party. You can always "wimp-out" and buy an assortment of ready-to-cook pizzas. I've surely done my share of this! Or you can try some of these suggestions.

The Crust:

Buy your pizza crust in the frozen foods section at the grocery or in the dairy case. This is easy and remarkably good. Or if you really want that homemade crust, try this one.

1	(1/4-ounce) package active dry yeast	1-1/2	cups plain flour
1/2	cup warm water (warm tap water, not hot water)	1/2	teaspoon salt
		1	tablespoon vegetable oil

Preheat oven to 450. In a small bowl, dissolve the yeast in the warm water, and set aside. In a large bowl, mix together flour, salt, and oil. Add the dissolved yeast, and mix well. Turn this mixture out onto a floured cutting board, and knead until it forms a smooth ball. Place the dough into a greased bowl, cover the bowl with a dish. Let rise in a warm place about 10-15 minutes. While the dough is rising, grease the pizza pan. Place the risen dough onto the greased pan, and pat out the dough gently until it fits the shape of your pan. Crimp edge to form a rim. Lightly brush crust with oil. Bake crust without toppings in the preheated oven on the lowest rack until the bottom of the

(continued on next page)

Top Scorers

crust is lightly browned, about 3 or 4 minutes. Spoon the pizza sauce evenly on the baked crust. Add meats and chopped vegetables to suit your taste, and bake 15 minutes at 450 degrees. Sprinkle with cheeses, and bake an additional 5 to 10 minutes or until cheeses have melted and crust is golden brown.

The Toppings:

The ingredients you use to top your pizza are only limited by the imagination. A few suggestions for the more traditional toppings are:

Meat or Seafood Toppings

Sliced pepperoni
Chopped cooked ham
Sliced cooked Canadian bacon
Crisp fried bacon, crumbled
Cooked ground beef

Cooked sausage
Anchovies
Cooked Italian sausage slices
Cooked shrimp

Vegetable and Other Toppings

Thin sliced or diced onion
Thin sliced or diced green pepper
Thin sliced or diced red pepper

Sliced or chopped fresh or canned mushrooms
Sliced black olives
Sliced green olives

Cheeses Grated and/or Sliced

Mozzarella
Provolone
Cheddar

Parmesan
Romano

(continued on next page)

Top Scorers

The Sauces:

Once again there are various approaches to your sauce, depending on time and inclination. You can take the short-cut and buy a thick spaghetti sauce to use. Or if you prefer to make a quick, simple sauce try this:

Ze Quic Sauce

1	(8-ounce) can tomato sauce	1/2	teaspoon garlic salt
1	(6-ounce) can tomato paste, if a slightly sweet taste is preferred; or another 8-ounce can tomato sauce, if a tart taste is preferred	1/2	teaspoon dried oregano

Mix all ingredients in a saucepan, and bring to a boil. Reduce heat to a simmer, and cook for about 5 minutes. Use about 1/2 cup per pizza. Any remaining sauce can be refrigerated or frozen for future use. Makes enough sauce for about 3 to 4 pizzas.

The spaghetti sauce recipe in this book makes a great sauce for pizzas. If you are making a number of pizzas, use this sauce, which can be made in advance (either refrigerated or frozen), and make an assortment of bowls filled with all of the topping ingredients. "Build" your pizzas from this assembly line of ingredients to suit all of your guests before they arrive, or better yet, let each guest "build" their own.

I probably should have added a drop cloth to the list of ingredients for the cheese and topping fallout!

Top Scorers

Devilish Chicken

Microwave Recipe.

4	chicken breast halves with ribs, skinned	1/2	teaspoon garlic powder
1/2	cup (1 stick) margarine, melted	1/4	teaspoon curry powder
1	teaspoon salt	1/4	teaspoon dry mustard
2	teaspoons Worcestershire sauce	14	teaspoon paprika
1	teaspoon oregano, crushed	2	drops Tabasco sauce
		White rice	

Lightly salt chicken pieces. In a small bowl, mix the melted margarine with the remaining ingredients. Dip the chicken pieces into the margarine mixture to thoroughly coat each piece. Place the chicken pieces into a greased, flat baking dish. Pour the remaining sauce over the chicken. Cover dish with waxed paper, and microwave on high for 8 minutes. Open microwave, baste, and turn baking dish 1/4 turn. Cook for another 8 minutes. Baste again. Serve chicken on top of rice with a small amount of sauce. Serves 2 to 4.

You can use a conventional oven to make this dish. Cook, uncovered, at 350 degrees for about 1 hour. Baste chicken as it cooks.

Top Scorers

Stir-Fry Chicken with Walnuts

1-1/3 pounds chicken breast	3 tablespoons vegetable oil, divided
3 tablespoons soy sauce	2 medium green peppers, cut into strips
2 teaspoons cornstarch	
2 tablespoons cooking sherry	1 bunch green onions, chopped with green tops
1 teaspoon ground ginger	
1 teaspoon sugar	1 cup walnut halves
1/2 teaspoon salt	Cooked white rice
1/2 teaspoon crushed red pepper	

Cut chicken into 1-inch pieces, and set aside. In a small bowl, stir together soy sauce and cornstarch. Then add sherry, ginger, sugar, salt, and red pepper; blend and set aside. Heat 2 tablespoons of the oil in a wok or large skillet until very hot, but not smoking. Stir-fry green peppers and green onions for 2 minutes; remove to a bowl. Add the remaining 1 tablespoon oil, and stir-fry walnuts until golden. Remove the walnuts to the bowl with the peppers and onions. Spray the pan with vegetable oil, or add a small amount of oil. Stir-fry 1/2 the chicken pieces until done; remove to a dish. Stir-fry remaining chicken until done. Return all the chicken to the pan, and pour the soy mixture over the chicken; stir to coat all pieces. When mixture is thick and bubbly, add walnuts and vegetables. Stir-fry 1 additional minute. Serve hot over hot white rice. Serves 4.

Top Scorers

The Wishbone

This recipe is given for 2 servings, but it can easily be multiplied for as many guests as you have invited. Have the sauce made and the ingredients sliced for smooth maneuvering at serving time.

To Make Sauce:

3	tablespoons margarine	2	drops Tabasco sauce
1/2	teaspoon salt	1	cup sharp Cheddar cheese, grated
2	tablespoons plain flour		
1	cup milk		

In a large skillet, melt the margarine; then stir in the salt and flour until smooth. Gradually add the milk, keeping the sauce smooth; cook until thickened, stirring constantly. Stir in the Tabasco sauce and the cheese until melted; set aside.

To Make the Main Dish:

2	English muffins, split and toasted	4	thin slices tomato
4	generous slices cooked chicken or turkey breast	4	slices bacon, fried crisp

Preheat broiler to 500 degrees. Grease a flat, ovenproof baking dish, and place two English muffins halves in the bottom. Add a slice of chicken on top of each muffin. Pour 1 cup of the hot cheese sauce over the chicken, dividing it evenly. Top with the tomato slices and crisp bacon. Place the ovenproof baking dish under the broiler until the sauce is bubbling. Serves 2.

Top Scorers

Chicken à la Jean

6	boneless and skinless chicken breast halves, unsalted	8	ounces sour cream
			Black pepper
2	(2.5-ounce) packages shaved ham or beef	4	strips bacon, cooked until 1/2 done
			Paprika
1	(10-1/2-ounce) can cream of mushroom soup		

Wash chicken, and drain on paper towels. Grease a 2-quart baking dish; then tear the meat into strips, and layer the bottom of the baking dish with meat strips. Place the chicken on the meat layer. In a small bowl, blend the mushroom soup with the sour cream, and pour over the chicken. Sprinkle with black pepper, and place the bacon strips on top; then sprinkle with paprika. Bake at 350 degrees for 45 minutes.

Quick-As-a-Snap Chicken Rolls by Jane

6	chicken breast halves, skinned and boned		Onion dip
		6	strips bacon

Salt
Pepper

Pound the chicken breasts until flat; then lightly sprinkle with salt and pepper on both sides. On the side of the chicken that is less smooth, spread about 1 teaspoon onion dip. Roll the chicken, and secure with a cocktail pick. Wrap the bacon around the rolled chicken, and secure. Bake in a cooking dish sprayed with oil at 350 degrees for about 45 minutes.

For a variation of the dish, add 1/2 peeled carrot (split the long way) and a green onion to the inside of the chicken roll. This gives you vegetables with their own dip built in.

Top Scorers

South Pacific Grilled Chicken

6	boneless chicken breast halves, skinned	2	tablespoons vinegar
3/4	cup soy sauce (lite can be used)	1	large garlic clove, minced
1/4	cup brown sugar	1	medium onion, sliced
1	tablespoon vegetable oil		Cooked white rice

Wash chicken, and drain; then score diagonally 4 times making cuts deep, but not cutting through the chicken. Place chicken in a flat glass dish. In a small bowl, combine the remaining ingredients; mix well to dissolve the sugar. Pour the sauce over the chicken, and turn chicken several times. Cover and refrigerate for 1 hour; turn twice. Reserve sauce after removing chicken. Cook chicken on a hot grill until it is done. While chicken is on the grill, simmer the remaining sauce until the onions are tender. Serve the hot sauce over hot rice topped with a chicken breast.

Mama's Cornish Hens

2	Cornish hens	1	celery rib
	Garlic salt	1	cup water
	Pepper	2	teaspoons chicken bouillon
	Lemon pepper marinade		
1/2	small onion		

Wash the Cornish hens, and pat dry with paper towel. Sprinkle each hen on the outside and in the cavity with garlic salt, pepper, and lemon pepper marinade. Place 1/2 of the onion and 1/2 of the celery rib in each hen cavity. Heat the water to boiling, then stir in the bouillon until dissolved. Pour the bouillon into the baking dish. Place the hens in the baking dish with the bouillon, and cover. Bake at 350 degrees for 1-1/2 hours. Uncover during the last 20 minutes of cooking time to brown.

Top Scorers

Trey's Grilled Fresh Catch

Fresh fish other than snapper can also be used.

2 red snapper fillets	1 small clove garlic, minced
Salt	
6 tablespoons margarine	4 green onions, divided
Juice of 2 large lemons	1 teaspoon Cavender's All Purpose Greek Seasoning
1/2 teaspoon Worcestershire sauce	

Wash fillets, and allow to drain; then salt on both sides. In a small saucepan, melt margarine with the lemon juice, Worcestershire sauce, garlic, and 2 green onions that are chopped (including the tops). Simmer for 2 minutes. Make a pan of aluminum foil with crumpled edges, for strength, that will hold the fish and the sauce. Put the foil pan on a hot grill; place the fillets in the pan, skin side down. Baste the fish with the sauce, and sprinkle the fillets with the Greek seasoning. Close the grill, and cook only until the fish flakes and is white in color. Baste several times while cooking. Just before serving, garnish with the remaining green onions and green tops that have been finely chopped.

Top Scorers

Super Shrimp

30	large shrimp	3/4	cup catsup
10	slices bacon, cut in 3 pieces each	1/4	cup lemon juice
		2	cloves garlic, mashed
Cocktail picks		1	tablespoon brown sugar
1/2	cup soy sauce	3	drops Tabasco sauce

Peel shrimp, and wash in 6 different rinses of cold water to clean. Wrap a 1/3 strip of bacon around each shrimp, and secure with a cocktail pick. In a large bowl, mix the soy, catsup, lemon juice, garlic, brown sugar, and Tabasco sauce. Add the wrapped shrimp to the sauce, and toss to coat. Cover the shrimp, and refrigerate for about 4 hours; stir several times. When ready to cook, place the shrimp in a flat baking dish, and broil until the bacon is crisp. This requires careful watching to prevent undercooking bacon, overcooking shrimp, or burning.

These'll disappear like a football under a pile-up on the goal line.

Top Scorers

Goal Post Seafood Kabobs

Shrimp
Scallops
Whole fresh mushrooms
Onions
Green pepper
Pineapple (optional)
1/4 cup vegetable oil

1/4 cup lemon juice
1/4 cup soy sauce
1/2 teaspoon salt
1/4 teaspoon pepper
1 slice bacon per skewer, or more if desired

Use fresh or frozen seafood. Peel and wash fresh shrimp in 6 rinses of cold water; drain. Rinse scallops, and drain. If using frozen seafood, allow it to thaw. Determine the number of shrimp and scallops to be used. Wash and cut mushrooms in half. Use very small whole onions, or larger onions cut to fit skewers. Cut green peppers into 1-inch squares and pineapple into chunks. Place the seafood, vegetables, and fruit in a bowl. Combine the oil, lemon juice, soy sauce, salt, and pepper in a small bowl; beat vigorously to blend. Pour the marinade over the seafood mixture; and refrigerate, covered, for about 2 hours. Stir the mixture occasionally. Fry bacon until it is almost done, but not crisp; cut into pieces to place on skewers. Use long metal skewers, and fill with alternating seafood, vegetables, fruit, and bacon. Cook about 4 inches from moderately hot coals for 6 minutes. Turn and cook for 4 to 6 minutes longer. The seafood cooks quickly; don't overcook.

These can also be served as appetizers. Soak wooden skewers in water overnight. Use the same directions—just make mini-kabobs.

Top Scorers

Cajun Boil

4	pounds fresh, unshelled shrimp (Crawfish can be substituted or mixed with the shrimp)	10	small whole onions, peeled
	Salt	4	ribs of celery, uncut and washed
3	ounces crab boil seasoning in bag	2	fresh lemons, sliced
		1	can beer (optional)
10	small to medium new, red potatoes, skin left on and washed	10	frozen 1/2 ears corn

Wash shrimp in 6 different washes of cold water to clean; drain. In a very large pot, add about 1-1/2 gallons water and salt to taste. (Actually, make it a little saltier than to taste since the ingredients all require more salt when boiled.) Bring the salted water to a hard boil; add crab boil seasoning, potatoes, onions, celery, lemons, and beer. Reduce heat to a gentle boil; cover and cook until potatoes are just tender. Bring water back to a hard boil; add corn and shrimp. Lower heat to a gentle boil; cook about 7 to 8 minutes until shrimp turn pink, and corn is tender. Drain and serve on a large, warm platter. Serves 6 or more.

This recipe is straight-down-the-middle fun to eat. Put lots of newspapers on the table with a stack of napkins, and plenty of butter for the corn and potatoes. Then dive-in! It's "right some good."

Top Scorers

Coach's Favorite Shrimp Thermidor

1 pound fresh shrimp	Dash cayenne pepper
1 cup fresh sliced mushrooms	2 cups milk
1-1/2 teaspoons salt, divided	1/2 cup Parmesan cheese, grated
1/2 cup margarine, divided	Ritz cracker crumbs
1/4 cup flour	Paprika
1/2 teaspoon dry mustard	

Peel and wash shrimp in 6 different rinses of cold water; drain. In a skillet, saute raw shrimp and mushrooms in 1/4 cup of the margarine for 5 minutes or until shrimp are pink in color. Sprinkle with 1 teaspoon of the salt. Remove shrimp and mushrooms; set aside. Add the remaining 1/4 cup margarine to the skillet, and melt. Blend in the flour until smooth; then add the remaining 1/2 teaspoon salt, dry mustard, and cayenne. Stirring constantly, gradually add milk, keeping the sauce smooth. Cook over medium heat, until thickened. Blend in the Parmesan and the shrimp mixture. Pour into a greased 2-quart baking dish. Cover the top with cracker crumbs; then sprinkle paprika for color. Bake at 350 degrees for about 30 minutes. Serves 4 to 6.

Top Scorers

No Substitutes Crab

1	pound white lump crabmeat	1/8	teaspoon cayenne pepper
1/3	cup margarine		Paprika
3	tablespoons lemon juice	6	parsley sprigs (optional)
1	teaspoon salt		

Remove any shell or cartilage from crabmeat. In a skillet, melt margarine; then stir in the lemon juice, salt, cayenne pepper, and crabmeat. Grease 6 individual crab shells or other suitable ovenproof containers, and fill each with the crab mixture. Sprinkle with paprika, and place the shells on a broiler pan about 4 inches from the heat source. Broil for 7 minutes until crab is hot but not dry. Place a parsley sprig in the center of each crab. Yield: 6.

Well, I'm sure you've had your share of crab dishes that taste like one poor little crab aimlessly wandered through 5 pounds of bread stuffing! No substitutes here; just pure lump crabmeat well seasoned.

Pat's Field Goal Fried Fish

Fish fillets, any type white fish suitable for frying
Zesty Italian salad dressing
Lemon Fish Fri
Vegetable oil
Salt, if needed

Place the fish fillets in a glass bowl with the salad dressing covering the fillets, then dredge in the Lemon Fish Fri to coat completely. Fry fillets in hot oil until done. Fish is cooked when the meat is white and flakes when tested with a fork. Drain on paper towel in a single layer.

Top Scorers

Hero Worship

Sometimes it's just hard to beat a really fantastic sandwich. Here are some suggestions. You pick the ones to run with!

Maximum Yardage

Whole loaf French or Italian bread
Mayonnaise
Mustard
Cotto salami, sliced thin

Onions, sliced very thin in rings and separated
Tomatoes, sliced thin
Mozzarella cheese, sliced thin

Slice the loaf of bread horizontally enough to open to fill with the ingredients. Place the opened loaf on a piece of aluminum foil. Spread one surface with mayonnaise, and the other with mustard. Layer with the remaining ingredients; then add another layer of salami on top. Wrap tightly in the foil, and heat at 350 degrees until the entire loaf is hot and the cheese has melted. Unwrap, and slice in generous "hunks."

If you're having a really big bash, ask a bakery to make a loaf several feet long to suit the number in your party. You may have to cut the loaf to get it in your oven. Then, after cooking, just place the ends back together to give that "long run for the goal" effect.

The Gutbuster

Polish sausage, cooked
Sauteed onion rings and green peppers, salted

Sourdough Subs

Top Scorers

Fist Sandwich

Virginia baked ham, sliced medium thickness
Imported Swiss cheese, sliced very thin

Kosher pickles, sliced thin
Kaiser rolls

The Pile-Up

Corned beef, sliced very thin and piled high
Provolone cheese, sliced thin

German mustard
Pumpernickel bread

Benchwarmer

Baked ham, sliced thin
Shredded lettuce, tomato, and onion with a few drops oil and vinegar, and sprinkled with salt

Individual French baguettes
Sharp Cheddar cheese, sliced thin

Additional cheeses that go with or on sandwiches:

Bousin
Fontina
Saga

Brie
Camembert
Havarti

Top Scorers

Roast in a Pocket

1-1/4	cups finely shredded lettuce	1	(3-ounce) package cream cheese, softened
1	medium tomato, chopped fine	1	tablespoon horseradish
			Mayonnaise
1	green onion, chopped fine	3	(6-inch) pita bread rounds, cut in half
3	tablespoons Italian salad dressing	6	ounces shaved roast beef

In a small bowl, combine the lettuce, tomato, and onion; then toss with the salad dressing. In another small bowl, mix the cream cheese with the horseradish, and enough mayonnaise to make it spread easily. Spread about 1-1/2 tablespoons of the mixture on the inside of each pita half. Fill the pockets with the roast beef and the salad mixture.

Referee's Shirt Sandwich by Julia Mae

1	4-1/2-ounce can deviled ham	1	tablespoon minced celery
1/2	teaspoon prepared mustard		Mayonnaise
		5	slices dark whole wheat bread
1-1/2	teaspoons prepared horseradish		
1	tablespoon chopped ripe olives	5	slices white bread

In a bowl, mix all ingredients except mayonnaise and breads. Lightly spread the mayonnaise on all the bread slices. Divide the sandwich mixture evenly on the whole wheat bread slices; then top with the white bread slices. Trim crusts, and slice in 3 or 4 long strips. Place the sandwiches on a serving plate, alternating the light bread and dark bread to give the black and white appearance of a referee's shirt. Yield: 15 to 20 small sandwiches.

Top Scorers

Yellow Flag Ham-It-Ups by Ann

Freeze the packages of rolls before making sandwiches for easy handling.

3	15-ounce packages finger rolls with poppy seeds on top	1	teaspoon Worcestershire sauce
1 to 2	tablespoons grated onion	1-1/2	tablespoons poppy seeds
1	cup (2 sticks) margarine, softened	1	12-ounce package sliced ham (more ham can be used for heartier sandwiches
3	tablespoons prepared mustard	12	thin slices Swiss cheese

Unwrap the frozen rolls, and slice the entire block of rolls in half horizontally. (Do not pull the individual rolls apart until serving time.) In a bowl, mix the onion, margarine, mustard, Worcestershire sauce, and poppy seeds until blended. Spread all of the roll surfaces with the mixture. Keep the ham in a stack, and cut through all the slices to get 6 pieces per slice of ham. This should be just wide enough to place a piece on each individual finger roll. Cut the cheese in the same way. Place a piece of ham and a piece of cheese on each finger roll. Replace the roll tops. The rolls can be heated several ways. Wrap the entire block of rolls in waxed paper, and microwave just long enough to melt the cheese (don't "nuke-it" and make rubber by microwaving too long!) Or you can microwave only a few at a time. You can also wrap the entire block, or a portion of it, in aluminum foil, and heat at 350 degrees in a conventional oven until the cheese is melted.

Great little make-ahead-of-time sandwiches. They can be refrigerated or frozen until time to serve; then they just seem to evaporate before your eyes as everyone pulls off a few. The referee and his yellow flag might come in handy....

Sideliners

The Salad Bowl

Salad needs to marinate overnight.

1	16-ounce can whole green beans, drained and washed	1	2-ounce jar sliced pimentos, drained
1	15-ounce can very young, small green peas, drained	1	4-ounce can chopped, peeled green chilies, undrained
1	17-ounce can small green lima beans, drained	1	4.5-ounce jar whole mushrooms, drained
1	14-ounce jar small, whole boiled onions, drained		

Marinade:

1	cup vegetable oil	1/2	teaspoon garlic salt
1/2	cup white vinegar	1/4	teaspoon pepper
1/2	teaspoon salt	1/4	teaspoon dry mustard
1/2	teaspoon sugar		

Place all marinade ingredients in a glass or plastic container that has a tight-fitting lid; put lid on container, and shake vigorously to blend. Gently place all of the vegetables in a large glass or plastic container that has a lid. Pour the marinade over the vegetables, and toss very gently. Refrigerate the salad overnight. Drain the vegetables to serve, but reserve the marinade. Any vegetables remaining can be returned to marinade and refrigerated for several days.

Sideliners

Tortellini Salad

1	cup uncooked Parmesan cheese stuffed tortellini	1/2	cup Cheddar cheese, julienne cut
1	cup uncooked spinach stuffed tortellini	1/2	cup Swiss cheese, julienne cut
2	ounces Pepperoni, julienne cut	1/2	cup stuffed green olives, sliced
1	cup small broccoli flowerets, cooked 2 minutes in microwave	8	small cherry tomatoes, halved
1/2	cup black olives, sliced	1/2	cup Parmesan cheese, grated

Dressing:

1	cup vegetable oil	1/2	teaspoon salt
1/2	cup vinegar	1/4	teaspoon dry mustard
1	teaspoon sugar	1/2	teaspoon ground oregano
1	teaspoon coarse black pepper	1/4	teaspoon crushed red pepper
1	small clove garlic, minced		

Cook both tortellinis as directed on their packages; drain. In a large bowl, mix all of the salad ingredients except the dressing ingredients. Toss gently to mix. In a small bowl, mix all of the dressing ingredients; beat vigorously to blend. Pour 1/2 of the dressing over the salad, and toss to mix. Serve the extra dressing on the side. Keep salad refrigerated, but allow the individual servings to come to room temperature. Serves 6.

Sideliners

Tom's Terrific Slaw

There's a secret to this recipe—how the cabbage is shredded! Select a hard, non-leafy cabbage, and cut it into quarters. To get long, thin shreds of cabbage, finely shred the quartered cabbage on the longest surface with a steel-blade vegetable slicer, or use a sharp knife and shred by hand. The slaw does not taste the same if it's chopped or coarse. The extra effort is worth it.

- 4 cups thinly shredded cabbage, packed firmly
- 1/2 teaspoon salt
- 1/2 teaspoon garlic salt
- 1/4 teaspoon black pepper
- 1/8 teaspoon crushed red pepper (optional)
- 1/2 teaspoon celery seed (do not omit)
- 2 to 2-1/2 tablespoons Wesson oil
- 1 tablespoon white vinegar

Place the shredded cabbage in a large bowl with room to toss. Sprinkle salt, garlic salt, black pepper, red pepper, and celery seed evenly on top of cabbage; then pour oil over the spices. Toss well to distribute spices and oil. Finally, add vinegar, and toss again. If slaw is too tart for your taste, add a pinch of sugar to "tone-down" the vinegar. Cover and refrigerate. Serves 4.

My father concocted this recipe years ago. It is often requested with seldom any left. If any remains, some people prefer it a day old after it has marinated. The recipe can be doubled or tripled. It appears to be a great mound of cabbage when you begin, but as you add the ingredients, it suddenly drops to half its volume! Don't despair; it's just packed and will serve more than you realize. The slaw can be used as a side dish or in sandwiches. For a party, shred the cabbage early in the day; then cover and refrigerate. Shortly before serving time, add the spices, oil, and vinegar to the already shredded cabbage.

I have repeated this recipe from my cookbook, **The Magnolia Collection.** *It's a natural for football parties.*

Sideliners

Dear's Cucumbers and Onions

2	medium cucumbers, peeled and sliced in thin rounds	White vinegar Salt and pepper
1	very large onion, sliced in rings	

Place the cucumbers and onions in a medium-size glass bowl. Add enough vinegar to barely cover the vegetables since the cucumbers will "weep" and increase the liquid. Salt generously, and pepper. Cover and refrigerate overnight. These will keep in the refrigerator for a week.

My grandmother whom I called "Dear" always had a bowl of these in her refrigerator during the summer. Great on a simple salad with fresh tomato slices or on a sandwich. By an interesting coincidence, my other grandmother marinated onion rings overnight in vinegar and salt to serve on hamburgers. I don't think I've ever had a hamburger as good hers since!

Logan's Blue Cheese Dressing

4	ounces blue cheese	2	tablespoons real sherry or cooking sherry
2	tablespoons water		
1/4	teaspoon garlic powder	1	cup mayonnaise

In a medium-size open bowl, mash the blue cheese with the water. Add a few drops more water if needed to make mixture stir. Mix in the remaining ingredients, and stir until smooth. Place dressing into a glass or plastic container with a tight-fitting lid, and refrigerate. Served chilled over lettuce, sliced fresh tomatoes, etc.

The dressing can also be used as a dip for fresh vegetables.

Sideliners

Pasta Primavera

1	pound linguine or fettucine	1/2	cup small broccoli flowerets
2	tablespoons salt	1/4	cup margarine
1	large clove garlic, split in half	1	cup whipping cream
		1/2	cup Parmesan cheese, grated
1	large carrot, peeled and julienne cut	1	teaspoon dill
1/2	green pepper, julienne cut	1/2	teaspoon salt
		1/4	teaspoon black pepper

Using a large pot, bring 4 quarts of water to a boil. Add the 2 tablespoons of salt and the garlic; then gradually add the pasta. Bring pasta to a boil; cover, and turn heat off. Allow pot to remain on the hot burner for 10 to 13 minutes; drain, and remove garlic. Spread the julienne cut carrots, green peppers, and broccoli in one layer in a glass baking dish. Microwave 2 minutes on high, or boil in a small amount of water for 2 minutes in a saucepan. In a large pot, melt margarine; then add the remaining ingredients. Stir to blend over low heat, and begin adding the drained pasta. Coat all the pasta with the sauce; then fold in the drained vegetables. Serve immediately. Serves 4 to 6.

Sideliners

Pasta Perfecto

This is a very light side-dish pasta.

Sauce:

- 3 tablespoons vegetable oil
- 2 large cloves garlic, crushed
- 1 (16-ounce) can tomatoes or 1 pound fresh, peeled tomatoes
- 1 teaspoon dried basil
- 1/2 teaspoon sugar
- Salt to taste

In a large skillet, heat oil; add the garlic, and cook until it begins to brown. Add the tomatoes including the juice (watch out for spattering), basil, and sugar. Reduce heat, and stir to begin breaking the tomatoes; salt to taste. Simmer, uncovered, about 30 minutes. Stir occasionally to break tomatoes and blend.

Pasta:

Vermicelli (thin spaghetti)
Water
Salt

Don't ask me how much vermicelli; I never seem to know. Anyway, add your desired amount of pasta to lots of boiling, salted water. Bring to a hard boil, and cover; turn the heat off, but allow the pot to remain on the hot burner for exactly 9 minutes. Drain pasta; either mix into the sauce, or pour the sauce on top of the pasta.

Sideliners

Sweet and Sour Green Beans

2	(16-ounce) cans whole green beans, drained	8	slices bacon
1	(8-ounce) can water chestnuts, drained and sliced thin	1/2	cup vinegar
		1/4	cup granulated sugar
		1	medium onion, sliced in rounds and separated

Place the drained green beans in a flat casserole dish, and top with the sliced water chestnuts. Fry bacon until very crisp. Reserve 1/4 cup drippings after removing bacon to cool. Combine the vinegar and sugar with the drippings; then bring to a boil. Pour the boiling sauce over the green beans. Crumble the bacon over the top, and place the onion ring slices evenly. Bake, uncovered, at 350 degrees for 30 minutes; then cover and bake another 30 minutes. Serves 6.

John's Bama Bell Peppers

4	bell or green peppers	1	cup bread crumbs
8	ounces sharp Cheddar cheese, grated	2	tablespoons margarine
1	cup milk		Salt and pepper to taste

After discarding the center seeds, wash and cut peppers into 1-inch pieces. Boil the pepper pieces in salted water for 5 to 10 minutes until tender. Drain peppers, and mix in remaining ingredients. Place mixture into a greased baking dish. Bake at 350 degrees for 30 minutes. Stir the mixture twice while it is cooking.

Sideliners

Beanie G. Beanpole's Baby Squash Deluxe

8	small yellow squash	1/2 to 1 cup sharp Cheddar cheese, grated
1	medium onion, chopped	Almond slivers, toasted
1	(10-1/2-ounce) can cream of celery or mushroom soup	

Optionals:
Green onions, chopped   Crisp bacon, crumbled
Peanuts, chopped

Wash squash, then cook whole in salted water with the onion until tender. While squash is cooking, pour the undiluted soup into a small saucepan, and heat until just bubbling. Drain water from squash and onion; then gently place the squash and onion on a warm platter. Pour the hot soup over the squash, and sprinkle the top with the cheese and almonds. Serves 4.

Quick, easy, and delicious. If there is any of this squash recipe left over after the first meal, make a casserole for another meal. Chop the leftovers, and add a beaten egg and bread crumbs to thicken. Pour into a greased baking dish, and top with grated cheese. Bake at 350 degrees until firm.

If you're curious about the title, Beanie's real name is Elizabeth! Her brother nicknamed her at an early age because she was as thin as a beanpole. That was certainly never one of my nicknames!

Sideliners

Fresh Astroturf

30 small spears fresh asparagus	3 tablespoons margarine, melted
1-1/2 cups water, divided	Juice of 1/2 to 1 lemon
1 teaspoon salt, divided (adjust to spear size and taste)	Black pepper
	Paprika
1 medium garlic clove, sliced in half	

Wash the asparagus; then snap the tender tops off the asparagus spears (use about the top 4 inches of the spear.) Set the bottom parts aside. In a saucepan, add 3/4 cup of the water and 1/2 teaspoon of the salt. Stand the asparagus spears upright in the pan (or slightly leaning) to keep only the bottoms of the asparagus in the water. Cover the pan, and bring water to a hard boil. Reduce heat to a gentle boil, and cook for 10 minutes (larger spears may require slightly longer to cook and more water.) While the tops are cooking, select 1/2 of the largest asparagus bottoms that were set aside. Using a vegetable peeler, remove the outside layer of the stalk, and cut the remaining inside stalk into 1-inch pieces. In a saucepan, add remaining 3/4 cup water, 1/2 teaspoon salt, garlic clove, and asparagus stalk pieces. Cover and bring to a hard boil; then reduce heat to a gentle boil. Cook about 8 minutes or until tender (do not allow all the water to evaporate; add more if needed.) Drain the cooked pieces, and puree in a blender or food processor along with the cooked garlic. Add the margarine and lemon juice; puree again. Drain the hot asparagus spears; place gently on a warm platter, and spoon the pureed sauce over the spears. Sprinkle with pepper and paprika.

The sauce does take a little extra time to make, but what a flavor difference! Same as afternoon practice, hard to do everyday; but it shows up on the scoreboard.

Sideliners

Genia's Green Beans Parmesan

1	(16-ounce) can French-style green beans, drained		Cracked black pepper
2	tablespoons margarine	4	crackers, crumbled (or more, if small)
1/3	cup Parmesan cheese, grated		

While green beans are draining, melt the margarine in a skillet. Add green beans, and saute over medium heat for 2 minutes. Mix in the Parmesan cheese, and continue to stir over heat for another minute. Sprinkle pepper to taste, and add crumbled crackers; toss to mix. Serves 3 to 4.

No Bullets Allowed

3 to 6 slices bacon, fried crisp
3 tablespoons margarine
1 (16-ounce) package frozen small green peas
2 cups coarsely shredded lettuce
1 large onion, sliced in rings
1 teaspoon granulated sugar
Garlic salt to taste
Black pepper to taste

In a large skillet, melt margarine; then stir-fry the frozen green peas, lettuce, and onion until lettuce is wilted. Add sugar, garlic salt, and pepper; mix well. Serve hot with the bacon crumbled on top. Serves 4 to 6.

Have you ever been served green peas so big and tough that they resembled green bullets? This recipe will redeem your faith in the tenderness and flavor of good green peas.

Sideliners

Mushrooms Parmesan

8 ounces fresh mushrooms, washed and stems removed	1/4 teaspoon black pepper
1/4 cup margarine	1/4 cup Italian or plain bread crumbs
2 tablespoons plain flour	1/4 cup Parmesan cheese, grated
1/2 cup Half and Half	
1/4 cup beef or chicken stock	

Preheat oven to 350 degrees. Grease a flat baking dish, and arrange the mushrooms stem side down. In a skillet, melt the margarine, and stir in the flour until smooth. Gradually stir in the Half and Half, and bring to a boil. Blend in the beef or chicken stock, and pepper; then return to a boil. Pour the hot sauce over the mushrooms, and sprinkle with the bread crumbs. Bake for 30 minutes; then sprinkle with the cheese. Bake an additional 5 minutes. Serves 4 to 6.

Joan's Cheesy Stuffed Potatoes

Microwave recipe.

- 4 medium baking potatoes
- 4 tablespoons margarine
- 1 (16-ounce) carton sour cream
- Salt and pepper to taste
- Sharp Cheddar cheese slices

Bake potatoes in a covered glass bowl in the microwave until soft in the center. Cut potatoes in half, and scoop out the center, leaving a firm shell. Mash the potato with the margarine and sour cream until smooth; add salt and pepper. Fill the potato shells, and place cheese slices on top. Microwave on high until potatoes are hot, and cheese is melted.

Sideliners

Out-of-Bounds Spuds

4	medium to large Idaho potatoes, washed and scrubbed	2	tablespoons fresh minced or dried chives
1/2	cup (1 stick) margarine, melted	1/8	teaspoon garlic powder
		1/2	teaspoon salt
		1/2	teaspoon black pepper
2	tablespoons fresh minced or dried parsley	1	teaspoon Worcestershire sauce

Bake potatoes according to your own taste—wrapped in foil on the grill or in the oven and baked at 350 degrees for 1 to 1-1/2 hours. If you prefer to use the microwave, place the potatoes in a glass bowl, and cover to bake. Follow your microwave cooking instructions for cooking time. While potatoes are baking, melt the margarine in a saucepan, and add the remaining ingredients. Beat the margarine mixture vigorously with a fork or wire whip to blend and dissolve all ingredients. When potatoes are done, split open and mash the inside of the potato; then spoon the margarine mixture onto the softened potato.

The flavor is out-of-bounds!

Sideliners

Greek Potatoes

5 medium Idaho potatoes, unpeeled	3/4 cup Half and Half
1-1/4 cups crumbled feta cheese	2 tablespoons margarine, melted
10 large stuffed green olives, sliced thin	1/4 teaspoon pepper
	1/2 teaspoon garlic salt

Garnish (optional):
1 medium green pepper, cut in strips   2 tablespoons margarine

Cook potatoes in boiling salted water until tender, about 25 minutes. Drain and cool potatoes; then peel. Cut into small 1/2-inch cubes. Combine potatoes with the remaining ingredients except the garnish, and gently toss to mix. Place into a greased flat baking dish. In a skillet, saute the green pepper strips in the 2 tablespoons margarine until slightly tender. Place pepper strips around the edge of baking dish. Bake at 350 degrees for 45 minutes.

Sideliners

Italian Hoppin' John

2	Italian sausages	1	cup cooked rice
2	(16-ounce) cans blackeyed peas		Salt to taste
			Pepper sauce (optional)
1	medium onion, minced		
1	small green onion, minced		

Cook sausages, and slice, reserve drippings. In a saucepan, mix all ingredients; then add about a tablespoon of the drippings for flavor. Serve the pepper sauce on the side for individual use.

No doubt this is a Southern Italian recipe!

In-a-Hurry Bean Skillet by Betty

1	medium green pepper	2	drops Tabasco sauce
1	medium onion	3/4	teaspoon garlic salt
2	tablespoons margarine	1/2	teaspoon prepared mustard
1	(15-ounce) can kidney beans, undrained		
1	(4-ounce) can mushroom pieces, undrained		

Cut green pepper and onion into 1/2 inch pieces. Use a large well-seasoned black iron skillet or other heavy skillet to melt the margarine. Add the undrained beans, undrained mushrooms, Tabasco sauce, garlic salt, and mustard. Bring to a boil; cover and reduce heat to simmer until most of the juice has cooked away. Serves 4 to 6.

The recipe can be doubled, and it can be made a day in advance.

Sideliners

Huevos Rancheros

There are as many different versions of this recipe as there are Mexican-food fans in a stadium. So try this one if you like huevos rancheros.

Flour tortilla or corn tostado shell, heated
1 tablespoon refried bean dip, heated
1 to 2 teaspoons sour cream, room temperature
Small amount of grated sharp Cheddar cheese

1 or 2 poached or fried eggs
More grated cheese
Salsa Verde, Red Salsa (see recipe on page 21), or taco sauce

On a plate, "build" this recipe as the ingredients are listed. Serve hot. Serves 1.

I like this as a brunch dish or as a simple supper.

Sideliners

Scrambled Hash Browns

3 slices bacon	1/2 to 3/4 cup sharp Cheddar cheese, grated
1 small onion, minced	1 drop Tabasco sauce
1 cup frozen hash browns	Salt to taste
1/4 teaspoon salt	
2 eggs	

Fry bacon in a skillet; remove bacon to drain, and reserve the drippings. Saute the onion and hash browns in 2 tablespoons of the drippings until tender. Sprinkle with the 1/4 teaspoon of salt. Beat eggs; then stir in the cheese, Tabasco sauce, and additional salt. Pour the egg mixture into the hot hash brown mixture, and scramble. Crumble the crisp bacon on top. Serves 2.

Use as a brunch dish for an early game or as a simple supper dish.

"Done Buttered Biscuits"

2 cups Bisquick	1 8-ounce carton sour cream
1/2 cup (1 stick) margarine, melted	

Preheat oven to 350 degrees. In a medium bowl, mix all ingredients until moistened, but do not beat. Drop by the spoonful into greased muffin cups. Bake for 12 to 15 minutes until lightly browned. Yield: 12 full-sized muffins.

Mexican Corn Bread

1-1/2 cups plain corn meal	2 tablespoons jalapeño relish
1 teaspoon salt	1 (16-ounce) can cream-style corn
3 teaspoons baking powder	1 cup sharp Cheddar cheese, grated
2 eggs, beaten	
2/3 cup vegetable oil	
1 cup sour cream	

Preheat oven to 350 degrees. Combine corn meal, salt, and baking powder; mix well. Add eggs, oil, and sour cream; stir until mixture is just blended. Stir in jalapeño relish and corn. Pour 1/2 batter into a greased 8-inch square baking dish. Cover with 1/2 of the cheese; repeat layers of batter and cheese. Bake in a preheated oven at 350 degrees for 35 to 40 minutes. Cut into squares.

Last Down

Chocolate Upside-Down Cake by Beth

No egg in this recipe!

1	cup plain flour	2	tablespoons margarine, melted
3/4	cup granulated white sugar	1/2	cup milk
2	teaspoons baking powder	1	teaspoon vanilla
1/4	teaspoon salt	1/2	cup chopped nuts

Sauce:

1/2	cup granulated white sugar	4	tablespoons cocoa
1/2	cup brown sugar	1	cup hot water

Preheat oven to 350 degrees; then grease an 8-inch square baking dish. In an electric mixer bowl, combine the first four ingredients with a fork. Add melted margarine, milk, and vanilla; beat on high for 4 minutes. Stir in the nuts by hand. Pour the batter into the greased pan. In another bowl, mix the sauce ingredients until blended. Pour the sauce over the unbaked cake. Bake in the preheated oven for 40 minutes. While the cake is baking, the chocolate sauce will invert in the dish, causing the cake to float on the sauce. Turn the hot cake out on a platter. Serve while hot with ice cream on top of the chocolate sauce.

Last Down

Elizabeth's Easy Coconut Cake

The cake is served in the baking dish.

1	(18.5-ounce) yellow, butter recipe cake mix	16	ounces sour cream
1	(15-ounce) can cream of coconut	8	ounces whipped topping
		12	ounces frozen coconut

Bake the cake as directed in a 9x13-inch baking dish. While the cake is baking, combine the cream of coconut and sour cream. Remove cake from the oven after baking time, and pierce holes in the top of the hot cake with a cocktail pick. Pour the cream of coconut mixture over the top of the hot cake. Allow the cake to cool; then spread with the whipped topping. Sprinkle the thawed coconut as a final layer. Cover and keep refrigerated.

Sometimes, actually often, I'm hopeless! I found the melted margarine for the cake mix in the microwave 10 minutes after I removed the beautiful baked cake from the oven!! Obviously, the margarine can be left out of that particular cake mix. I continued with my recipe for the remaining ingredients for a great tasting cake. Amazing...

Chocolate Spiders

1	(6-ounce) package real chocolate chips	6	ounces whole or slivered almonds
1	(3-ounce) can chow mein noodles		

Place the chocolate chips in a 2-quart glass baking dish. Heat in the microwave on level 6 for 3 to 3-1/2 minutes, or until melted. Chips may not appear melted until stirred. Add the noodles, and almonds; continue to stir until all the ingredients are chocolate coated. Drop by teaspoons onto waxed paper. Place in the refrigerator to get firm. Yield: 40.

Last Down

Time-Out Cherry Dessert

1 (1 pound 5 ounce) can cherry pie filling	1/2 cup (1 stick) margarine, melted
1 (9-ounce) box white cake mix (1 layer size)	3/4 cup pecans, chopped

Preheat oven to 350 degrees. Grease a 2-quart or 8-inch square baking dish; then evenly spread the cherry pie filling in the bottom. Sift the dry cake mix, evenly, over the cherry filling. Drizzle the melted margarine over the cake mix as evenly as possible; it will be a little spotty in places. Top with the pecans, and bake for 40 minutes.

Quick to make, easy to transport, and quick to be eaten.

Cherry Crumb Pie

3/4 cup granulated sugar	1 tablespoon margarine
2-1/2 tablespoons cornstarch	1 unbaked 9-inch pie crust
Scant 1/8 teaspoon salt	
1 (16-ounce) can water-packed pie cherries, undrained	

Crumb topping:

1 cup plain flour	1/3 cup margarine
1/2 cup granulated sugar	

In a saucepan, combine sugar, cornstarch, and salt; mix well. Gradually stir in the juice from the cherries until mixture is smooth. Cook and stir over medium heat until mixture is thick and clear. Add margarine, and stir until blended; then add the cherries. Pour pie filling into the unbaked pie crust. In a food processor, blender, or mixer, combine the crumb topping ingredients. Sprinkle the crumb topping on the pie filling. Bake at 375 degrees for 40 minutes. Serves 8.

Last Down

Choc-O-Lotty Pie

This recipe makes 2 pies. Prepare one day before serving. Save the plastic cover that protects the pie crusts.

1/2	gallon vanilla ice cream	2	chocolate cookie pie crusts
1	cup pecans, chopped and toasted		More toasted large pecan pieces to decorate
Chocolate syrup			

Place the ice cream into a large bowl; soften just enough to stir in the 1 cup toasted chopped pecans. Add enough chocolate syrup to make a marbled effect in the ice cream. Pour 1/2 of the ice cream mixture into each pie shell, and decorate the tops with the large pecan pieces. Invert the plastic pie shell covers over the pies; freeze overnight. Pies will stack in the freezer to save space. Yield: 2 pies.

Now, how could you possibly miss with this one?

Leonard's Japanese Fruit Pie

1/2	cup (1 stick) margarine, melted	1	cup pecans, chopped
1	cup granulated white sugar	1	cup raisins
		2	tablespoons vinegar
4	eggs, beaten	1	teaspoon vanilla
1	cup fresh or frozen coconut (do not use canned	1	unbaked 9-inch pie crust
		Sweetened whipped cream or commercial whipped topping	

Preheat oven to 300 degrees. In a bowl, beat the melted margarine and sugar until blended. Beat in the eggs; then stir in the coconut, pecans, raisins, vinegar, and vanilla. Mix well; pour into the unbaked pie crust. Bake for 50 minutes. Serve with whipped cream on each slice.

Last Down

Pecan Crispies by Jo

1/3 of a 1 pound box plain graham cracker cookies
1 cup (2 sticks) margarine
1/2 cup granulated white sugar
1-1/2 cups pecans, chopped

Preheat oven to 350 degrees. Separate cookies, and place side-by-side on a greased cookie sheet so that cookies touch. In a saucepan, melt margarine, and stir in the sugar. Bring the mixture to a boil, and cook for 1 minute. Remove from heat; mix in the pecans. Pour the hot mixture over the cookies, and bake in the oven for 9 to 10 minutes. Remove cookies immediately from the pan to waxed paper to cool.

These shiny cookies glisten like a football in the afternoon sun when you know the catch will be good!

Lou's Pecan Pie Squares

1 cup vegetable shortening
1 cup brown sugar, packed
1 teaspoon salt, divided
2 cups plain flour
3 eggs
1/2 cup granulated white sugar
1 cup corn syrup
1-1/2 cups whole pecans

Preheat oven to 350 degrees. In a food processor or electric mixer, cream shortening, brown sugar, and 1/2 teaspoon of the salt; then add flour and mix. Grease a 9 x 13-inch baking pan, and pat this mixture into the bottom. Bake for 10 minutes. While crust is baking, add the eggs to the mixer bowl along with the white sugar, corn syrup, and the remaining 1/2 teaspoon salt. Mix until all ingredients are well blended; then stir in the pecans by hand. Pour the pecan mixture over the cooked crust, and bake for 15 minutes at 350 degrees. Reduce heat to 275 degrees, and bake for about 15 to 20 minutes until set. Allow to cool before cutting into squares.

Last Down

Nutty Cheesecake Bars

2	packages refrigerated crescent rolls	1	egg, separated
2	(8-ounce) packages cream cheese, softened	1	tablespoon lemon juice
		1/2	cup pecans, chopped
3/4	cup granulated sugar, divided		

Preheat oven to 350 degrees. Open both packages of rolls, unroll, and allow to come to room temperature. Stretch out the dough in the first package to fit flat in the bottom of a greased 9x13-inch baking pan. Press the seams together to form a solid crust of dough. In an electric mixer, combine the cream cheese and 1/2 cup of the sugar until smooth. Mix in the egg yolk and lemon juice; then spread over the dough. Top with the second package of rolls that have been stretched and the seams sealed like the first package. Whip the egg white with a fork or whisk until frothy; then brush top of dough with whipped egg white. Mix the remaining 1/4 cup sugar with the pecans, and sprinkle on top. Bake for 25 minutes. Cool before cutting into squares. Store in the refrigerator.

These might not make it through the first quarter...

Cappuccino Chocolate Cookies

2 squares (2 ounces) unsweetened chocolate	1 teaspoon water
2 cups plain flour	1/2 cup vegetable shortening
1/2 teaspoon ground cinnamon	1/2 cup margarine, softened
1/4 teaspoon salt	1/2 cup granulated white sugar
1 tablespoon instant coffee crystals	1/2 cup brown sugar, packed
	1 egg, beaten

Chocolate Dip:

1/2 cup semi-sweet real chocolate chips	1 tablespoon vegetable shortening

In a small saucepan, heat and stir the unsweetened chocolate squares until just melted. Remove from heat immediately, and allow to cool. In a bowl, combine flour, cinnamon, and salt. In a cup, mix coffee crystals and the water. In an electric mixer, beat the 1/2 cup shortening, margarine, white sugar, and brown sugar until fluffy. Then add coffee mixture, melted chocolate, and egg; beat for 2 minutes. Add the flour mixture, and beat for another 2 to 4 minutes. Cover bowl, and refrigerate for about 1 hour, or until easy to handle. On waxed paper, form 2 rolls about 7 inches long; wrap in the paper, and refrigerate for at least 6 hours or overnight. Preheat oven to 350 degrees. Cut into thin 1/4-inch slices. Place slices on an ungreased cookie sheet, and bake for 12 to 16 minutes or until edges are firm and lightly browned. Allow to cool completely.

To dip: in a heavy small saucepan, heat and stir chocolate chips and the 1 tablespoon shortening on low heat until melted. Dip one half of each cookie into the chocolate; then place on waxed paper to allow chocolate to set. If the chocolate dipping mixture is not thin enough, add 1 or 2 more tablespoons of melted shortening to the chocolate. Yield: 50.

Last Down

Blueberry Nut Torte by Scotty

No baking needed to make this dessert. Do make it the day before serving.

1/2	cup granulated sugar	2	cups pecans, chopped
8	ounces cream cheese, softened	1/2	pint whipping cream
1	tablespoon milk	1	(15-ounce) can blueberries, undrained
1	cup whipped topping		
2	graham cracker crumb ready-made pie crusts		

In a mixer, blend the sugar, cream cheese, milk, and whipped topping. Spread the mixture, evenly divided, between both pie crusts. Sprinkle the chopped pecans for the next layer. In a small bowl, whip the cream, and lightly sweeten to taste. Spoon the whipped cream over the pecans, and gently spread. Finally, spoon the blueberries and some of their juice over the top. Cover and refrigerate overnight. Serves 16.

Helen's Chocolate Strawberry Drizzle

1	Sara Lee frozen pound cake	1/2	gallon vanilla ice cream (use the block type)
2	pints fresh strawberries, washed, hulled, and drained		Chocolate syrup

Slice the pound cake into 1/4-inch to 1/2-inch slices, allowing 2 slices per serving. Slice 8 to 12 strawberries per serving. Place 1 slice cake on each dessert plate (you can use disposable china, sometimes called paper plates); then add half the strawberry slices. Cut the ice cream into a 1/4-inch slice, and place on the strawberries. Drizzle the chocolate syrup over the ice cream in your favorite running pattern. Repeat the layers; then wipe 'em out with your spoon!!

Last Down

The Point Is—Good!

1 quart fresh strawberries (frozen may be used)	1 (10-ounce) package Lorna Doone cookies
1 (1 pound) package frozen raspberries	1/2 pint whipping cream
Granulated sugar to taste	
2 tablespoons Kirsch or other fruit liqueur (optional)	

Wash and hull the strawberries; then drain. Slice the strawberries into a saucepan, and add the frozen raspberries. Heat and stir the fruit only until the juices begin to run. Sweeten the fruit to taste; then stir in the liqueur. Whip cream in a cold bowl with cold electric mixer beaters; add sugar to taste. Place 4 cookies on each individual dessert plate. Add 1 or 2 tablespoons fruit, and top with whipped cream; repeat the layers. Serve immediately to keep the cookies crisp. Serves 4 to 6.

The Center's Favorite— Ice Cream with Praline Sauce

5 tablespoons margarine	1/2 cup Half and Half
1 cup brown sugar, packed	1 cup pecans, chopped
	Vanilla ice cream

In a saucepan, melt margarine, and add brown sugar. Cook over low heat, stirring constantly, for about 5 to 7 minutes. Remove from heat, and gradually stir in the Half and Half. Return to heat, and cook for 1 minute. Fold in the pecans, and stir. Serve hot over ice cream. The sauce can be cooled and refrigerated. Yield: 1-1/2 cups

This brings thoughts of that much sought-after "sweet" city—New Orleans.

Last Down

Ellen's Chocolate Brandy Melt

Microwave recipe.

1 large package (12-ounces) semi-sweet real chocolate chips	1/4 cup brandy or liqueur of choice
2 tablespoons Half and Half	

In a small glass bowl, microwave the chocolate chips at medium-high (70%) until chocolate is melted, about 2 to 4 minutes. Blend in the Half and Half and brandy. Serve warm for dipping.

Dipping Choices:
Strawberries
Pineapple chunks
Mandarin oranges
Fresh orange sections
Banana chunks (sprinkled with lemon juice)
Lady fingers, split
Pound cake fingers
Angel food fingers

Brad's Purple Cow

Frosted tall glass
Vanilla ice cream

Frozen reconstituted apple-grape juice

Fill the frosted glass with ice cream, and slowly pour grape juice over the top.

Index

Appetizers
Baked Brie in
Sourdough Bread 9
Bison Airfoils!,
Dorothy's 11
Brandied Shrimp 18
Chinese Pecans by Jean 22
Clock-Stopper
Chicken Tidbits...............14
Coins for the Toss
by Joan 14
First Downers 23
Forward Pass Spread,
Almand's.....................17
Goal Line Wings 22
Holy Smoke!..................12
Looks Bad Tastes Great
Dip by Betty 15
Monterey Quesadillas.......20
Mystery Crab and
Shrimp, Mary's 24
Pecan Confetti 19
Prairie Fire 16
Quesadillas Caliente.........20
Rah Rah's.....................17
Red Salsa 21
Referee Revenge.............10
Salsa Verde...................21
Scallop Ceviche..............19
Short Punts...................16
Surprise Wraps, Elmore's..18
Texas Crabgrass.............13
Top-Scoring
Mushrooms, David's 12
Wilson's Popcorn Bowl....23

Beverages
Canadian Coffee.............26
Hail Caesar!!.................26
Instant Replay, Jay's........24
Personal "Fowl"............27
Polar Pick-Me-Up...........25
Red River Red-Eye..........25
Straight-Down-the-Middle
Breezie, Jay Scott's.........25

Breads
Baked Brie in
Sourdough Bread.............9
"Done Buttered Biscuits"...78
First Downers................23
Mexican Corn Bread 79

Desserts
Cakes
Chocolate Upside-Down
Cake by Beth 81
Easy Coconut Cake,
Elizabeth's...................82
Time-Out Cherry Dessert...83
Cookies
Cappuccino Chocolate
Cookies......................87
Chocolate Spiders 82

Index

Nutty Cheesecake Bars.....86
Pecan Crispies by Jo........85
Pecan Pie Squares, Lou's..85
Ice Cream
Ice Cream with Praline
Sauce, The Center's
Favorite......................89
Purple Cow, Brad's........90
Just Desserts
Blueberry Nut Torte
by Scotty.....................88
Chocolate Brandy Melt,
Ellen's........................90
Chocolate Strawberry
Drizzle, Helen's.............88
Point Is—Good, The.......89
Pies
Cherry Crumb Pie...........83
Choc-O-Lotty Pie............84
Japanese Fruit Pie,
Leonard's....................84

Eggs
Huevos Rancheros..........77
Scrambled Hash Browns...78

Meats
Beef
Bar-B-Que Brisket
by Beverly...................42
Camp Stew, Cis's
Quick Crockpot.............37
Chili, Ann's Homemade....38
Chili, Joe's Wild
and Wooly...................36
Looks Bad Tastes Great
Dip by Betty................15

Pile-Up, The.................59
Roast in a Pocket...........60
Spaghetti, First and Ten....34
Steak, Hit-'Em-a-Lick......33
Steak, Hula..................31
Steak, Over-the-Top........32
Steaks, Quarterback Club..29
Steak, Scrimmage Line.....33
Pork
Ahhh! Pizzas...........44-46
Barbecue for the Fans.......39
Benchwarmer, The.........59
Camp Stew, Cis's
Quick Crockpot.............37
Fist Sandwich...............59
Gutbuster, The..............58
Ham-It-Ups by Ann,
Yellow Flag..................61
Maximum Yardage..........58
Pile-Up, The.................59
Referee's Shirt Sandwich
by Julia Mae.................60
Running Back Ribs.........40
Stick to Ya' Ribs
Linebacker Soup............43
Poultry
Bison Airfoils,
Dorothy's....................11
Camp Stew, Cis's
Quick Crockpot.............37
Chicken à la Jean...........50
Clock-Stopper
Chicken Tidbits.............14
Cornish Hens, Mama's.....51
Devilish Chicken............47
Goal Line Wings............22

Index

Quick-As-a-Snap
Chicken Rolls by Jane 50
Referee Revenge 10
South Pacific
Grilled Chicken.............. 51
Stir-Fry Chicken with
Walnuts...................... 48
Wishbone, The 49

Seafood
Brandied Shrimp 18
Cajun Boil 55
Coach's Favorite
Shrimp Thermidor 56
Field Goal Fried Fish,
Pat's......................... 57
Goal Post Seafood
Kabobs 54
Grilled Fresh Catch,
Trey's 52
Mystery Crab and Shrimp,
Mary's 24
No Substitutes Crab 57
Scallop Ceviche............. 19
Short Punts 16
Super Shrimp................ 53
Texas Crabgrass............. 13

Wieners
Gutbuster, The 58
Holy Smoke! 12
Rah Rah's 17

Pasta
Cooking the Pasta 35
Pasta Perfecto................ 68
Pasta Primavera 67

Spaghetti, First and Ten 34
Tortellini Salad.............. 64

Salads
Blue Cheese Dressing....... 66
Cucumbers and Onions,
Dear's........................ 66
Mystery Crab and Shrimp,
Mary's 24
Salad Bowl, The 63
Slaw, Tom's Terrific........ 65
Tortellini Salad 64

Sandwiches—
"Hero Worship"
Benchwarmer 59
Fist Sandwich................ 59
Gutbuster, The............... 58
Ham-It-Ups by Ann,
Yellow Flag 61
Maximum Yardage.......... 58
Pile-Up, The 59
Referee's Shirt Sandwich
by Julia Mae 60
Roast in a Pocket............ 60

Sauces
Bar-B-Que Brisket Sauce
by Beverly................... 42
Lazy Acres Bar-B-Que
Sauce, Pop's................. 41
Long Pass Barbecue
Sauce........................ 40
Quick Barbecue Sauce 39

93

Index

Vegetables
Asparagus
Fresh Astroturf 71
Beans
In-a-Hurry Bean Skillet..... 76
Prairie Fire 16
Green Beans
Green Beans Parmesan,
Genia's 72
Sweet and Sour
Green Beans 69
Mushrooms
Mushrooms Parmesan 73
Top-Scoring Mushrooms,
David's 12
Peas
Italian Hoppin' John 76
No Bullets Allowed 72
Peppers
Bama Bell Peppers,
John's........................ 69
Potatoes
Cheesy Stuffed Potatoes,
Joan's........................ 73
Greek Potatoes............... 75
Out-of-Bounds Spuds 74
Stick to 'Ya Ribs
Linebacker Soup 43
Spinach
Texas Crabgrass 13
Squash
Baby Squash Deluxe,
Beanie G. Beanpole's....... 70

Pigskin Parties, P.O. Box 869, Millbrook, AL 36054

Please send me _____ copies of *Pigskin Parties*.
(Includes Postage and Handling)   @ $ 8.50 each_____
[Or 3 for $20.85 plus $3.00 postage]   _____
Alabama Residents add 4% sales tax   @ .28 each_____
Gift Wrap   @ .75 each_____
                                    Total Enclosed_____
Print Name_____
Address_____
City_____State_____Zip_____

Checks to: *Pigskin Parties* or Chg. to: Visa _____ MC _____
Print Name_____ Exp. Date_____
Acc./# _____ Signature_____

— —

Pigskin Parties, P.O. Box 869, Millbrook, AL 36054

Please send me _____ copies of *Pigskin Parties*.
(Includes Postage and Handling)   @ $ 8.50 each_____
[Or 3 for $20.85 plus $3.00 postage]   _____
Alabama Residents add 4% sales tax   @ .28 each_____
Gift Wrap   @ .75 each_____
                                    Total Enclosed_____
Print Name_____
Address_____
City_____State_____Zip_____

Checks to: *Pigskin Parties* or Chg. to: Visa _____ MC _____
Print Name_____ Exp. Date_____
Acc./# _____ Signature_____

— —

Pigskin Parties, P.O. Box 869, Millbrook, AL 36054

Please send me _____ copies of *Pigskin Parties*.
(Includes Postage and Handling)   @ $ 8.50 each_____
[Or 3 for $20.85 plus $3.00 postage]   _____
Alabama Residents add 4% sales tax   @ .28 each_____
Gift Wrap   @ .75 each_____
                                    Total Enclosed_____
Print Name_____
Address_____
City_____State_____Zip_____

Checks to: *Pigskin Parties* or Chg. to: Visa _____ MC _____
Print Name_____ Exp. Date_____
Acc./# _____ Signature_____